# MARIA PAVLOVSKA

## REACTION

### DRAWING CYCLES 2005-2015

DRAWING ROOMS
**VICTORY HALL PRESS**

# MARIA PAVLOVSKA

## REACTION

**DRAWING CYCLES** 2005-2015

Edited by James Pustorino

*Maria Pavlovska*
*2006*

*"Art is nothing else than the pure document of the time we live in. Drawing remains an intimate, honest and powerful research."*

- Maria Pavlovska

# REACTION

Drawing, like poetry, can communicate the immeasurable depth of our thoughts, emotion and experience through a language that is often most precise when expressed in its most abstracted form. Maria Pavlovska's drawings engage this language, exploring the full range of her internal life even as her line and brush-stroke explore from the sensitive to the explosive, from freedom to order.

Maria's work carries the same intense, honest, dedicated focus that is so clearly evident in her personality. She has developed the ability to communicate deeply through the pure linear, gestural movements that compose her images. The emphatic energy of her artworks seems spontaneous, but is actually a result of a contemplated study, a build-up of actions and responses taking place within the work over a period of time. A canvas or series of drawings may take months to be fully realized, and carries that concentration of thought and action.

These cycles of small drawings are notes to herself, put down on paper over a span of ten years. They have an intimate power; she will often term them 'diaries'. Specific without depiction, they are images that can be read and appreciated over time, something a person wants to keep close and refer to again and again. Just as sonnets or song cycles create strings of poetic imagery, each drawing here adds to the next like a bead on a chain, or a part of a story, a page of a book.

This book, then, can be said to complete these collected sets of drawings, arranging them in a format that allows for such appreciation and becomes a part of her process. Created throughout the decade of Maria's shift from her native Macedonia to establish herself as an artist in the United States, they embody her personal struggles and aspirations. As Maria continues to gain attention from her fellow artists and curators and gallerists in the New York City area, she remains very true to her heritage, upbringing and her unique artistic direction.

James Pustorino

Director, DRAWING ROOMS

2006 - 2007 objects

oil, pen and pencil on cardboard

4 1/2 x 9 3/4 inches each / 11.5 x 24.5 cm

15
марта
Павловская
2006
сент
ент
рм

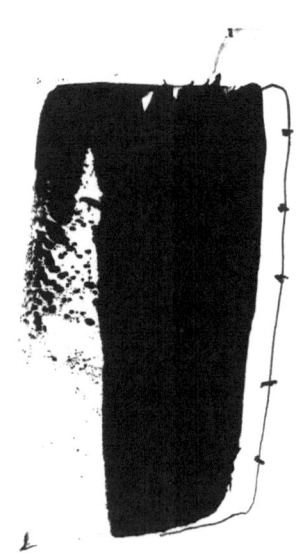

Marta Ranovska, Castro
2005
septen
uri too
rim og
tropski

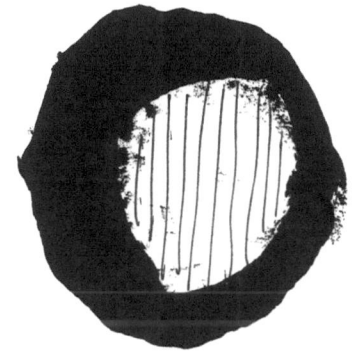

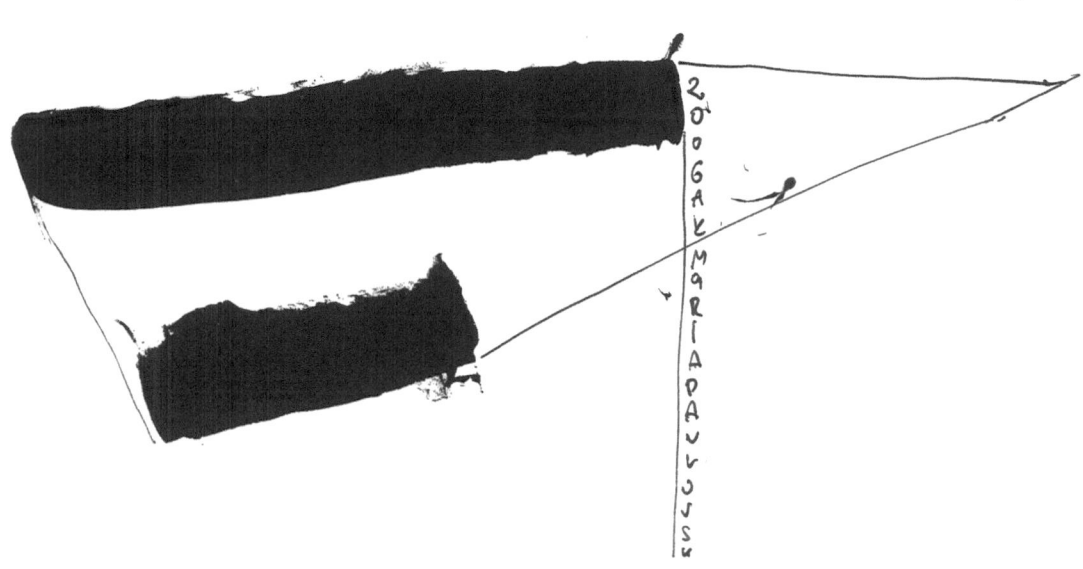

2006AKMARIAPAVLOVSK

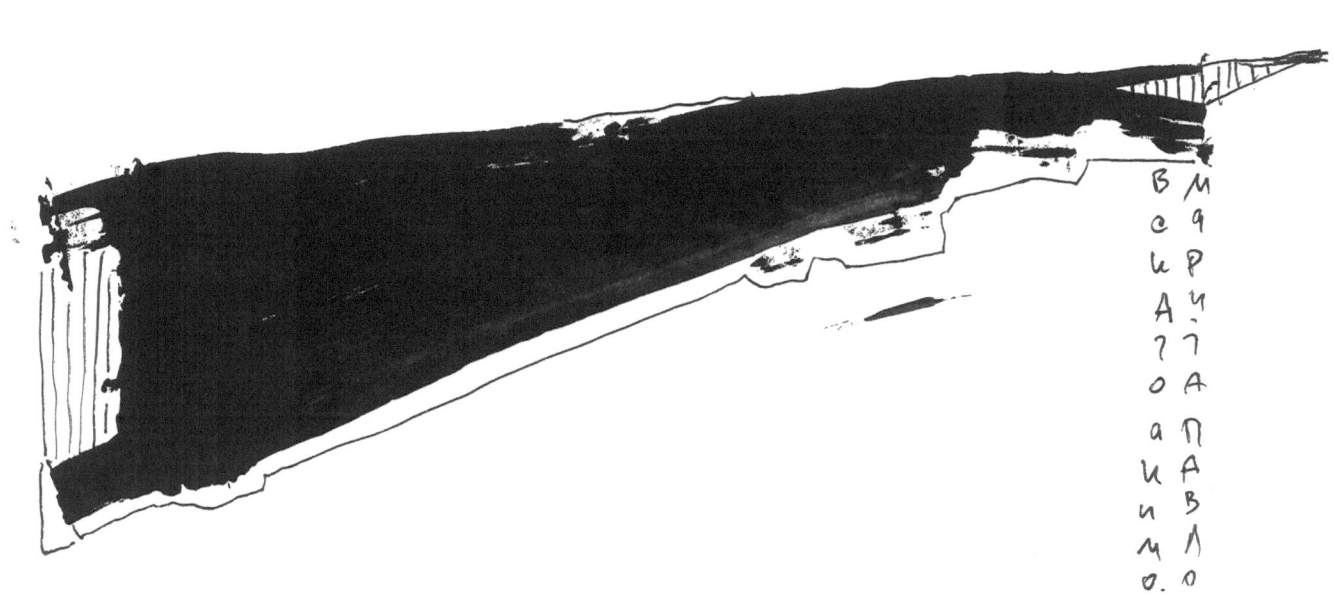

Все
с
к
А?
о
а
и
м
о.

Мя
Р
ч
Т
А
П
А
В
Л
о

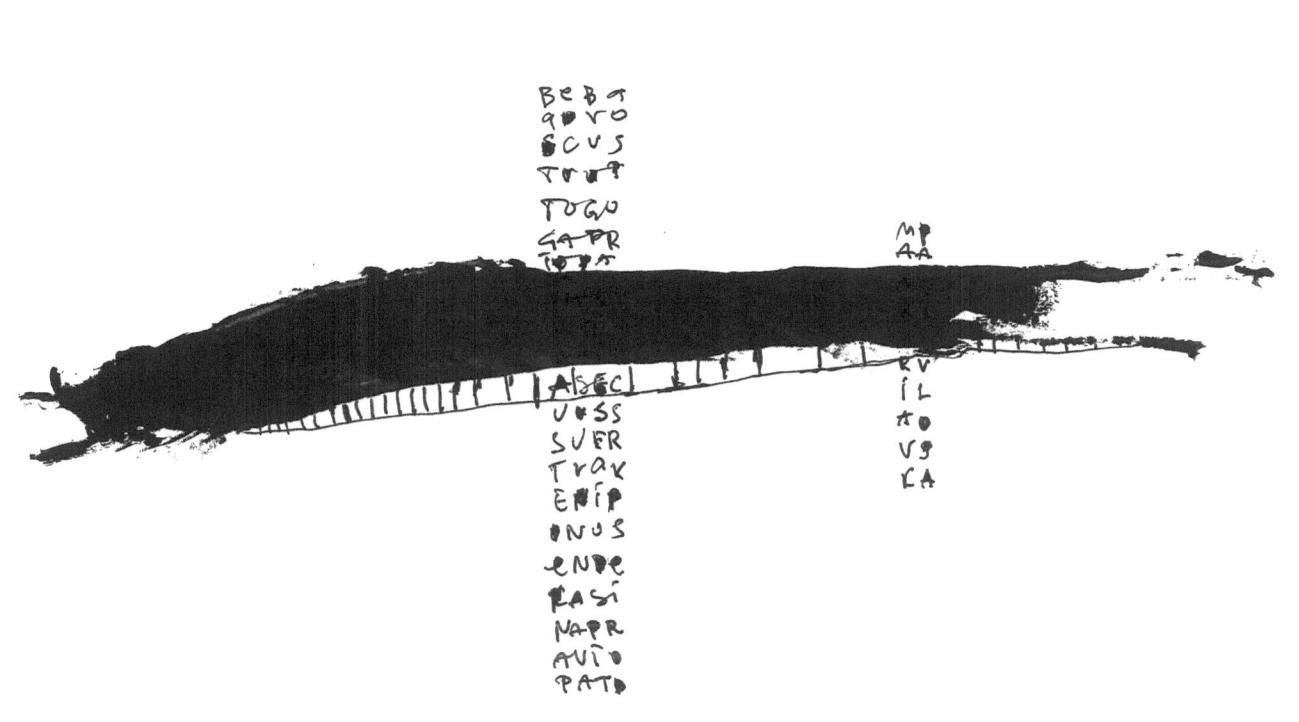

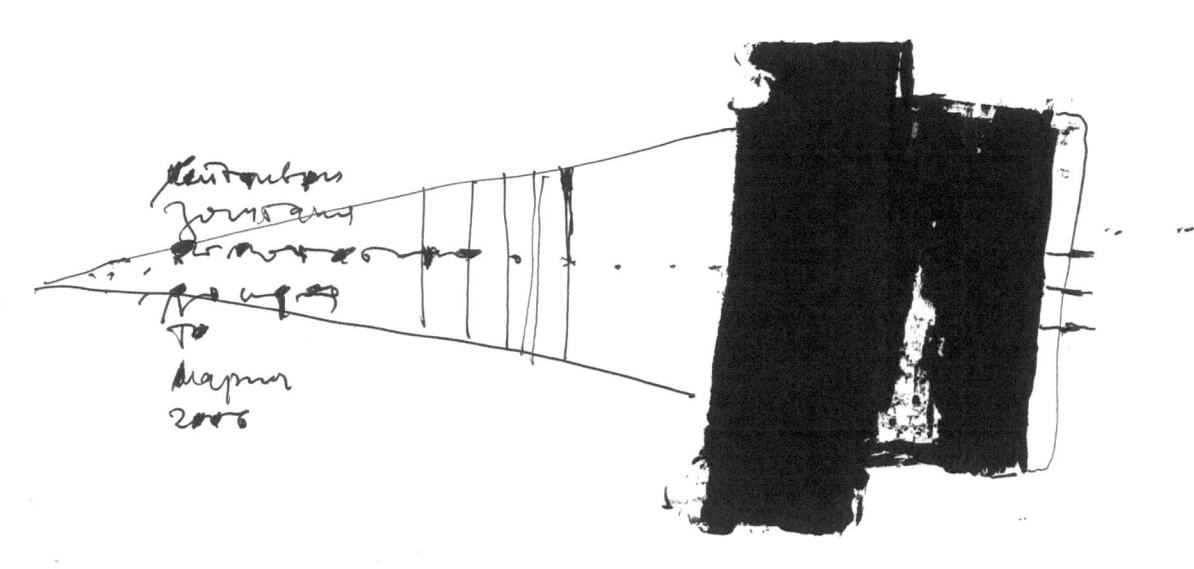

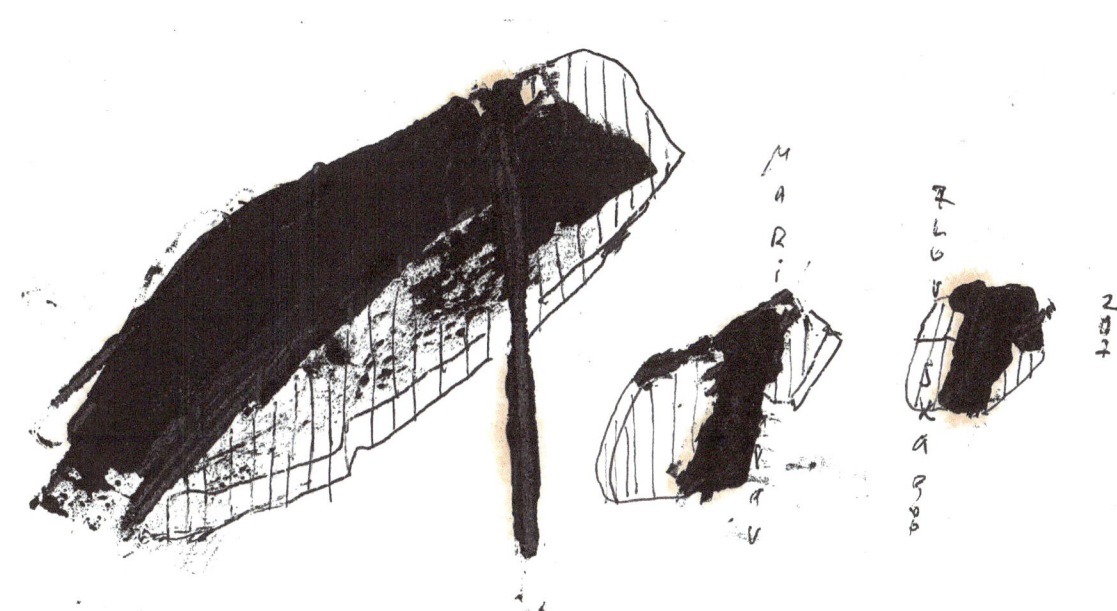

MARI
'AU

7
6
U
BRK
A
P00

2007

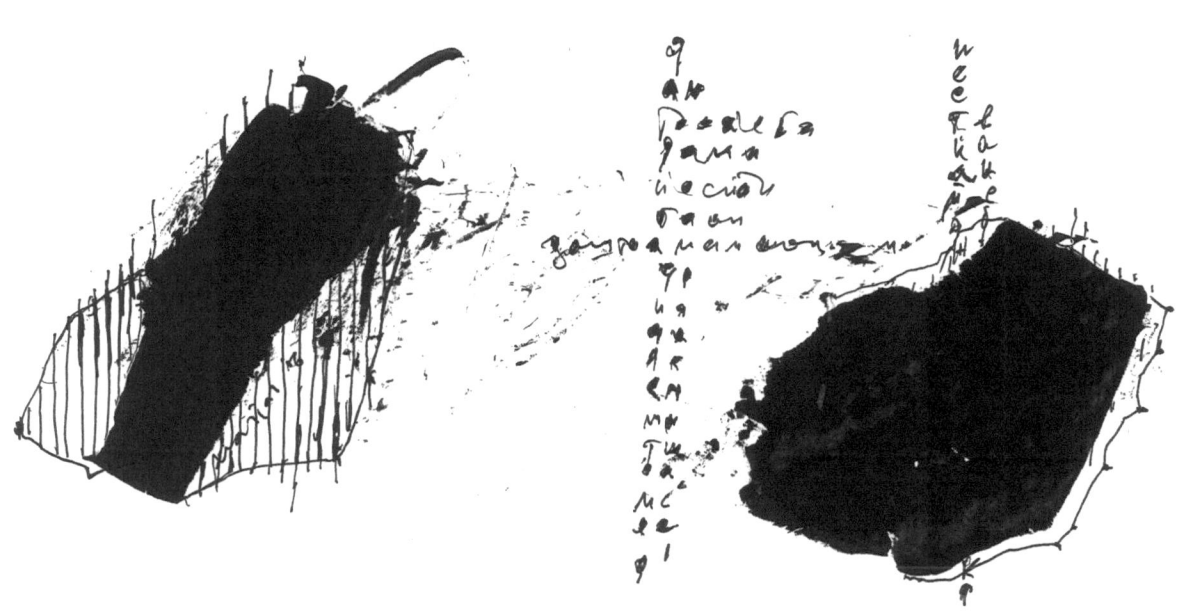

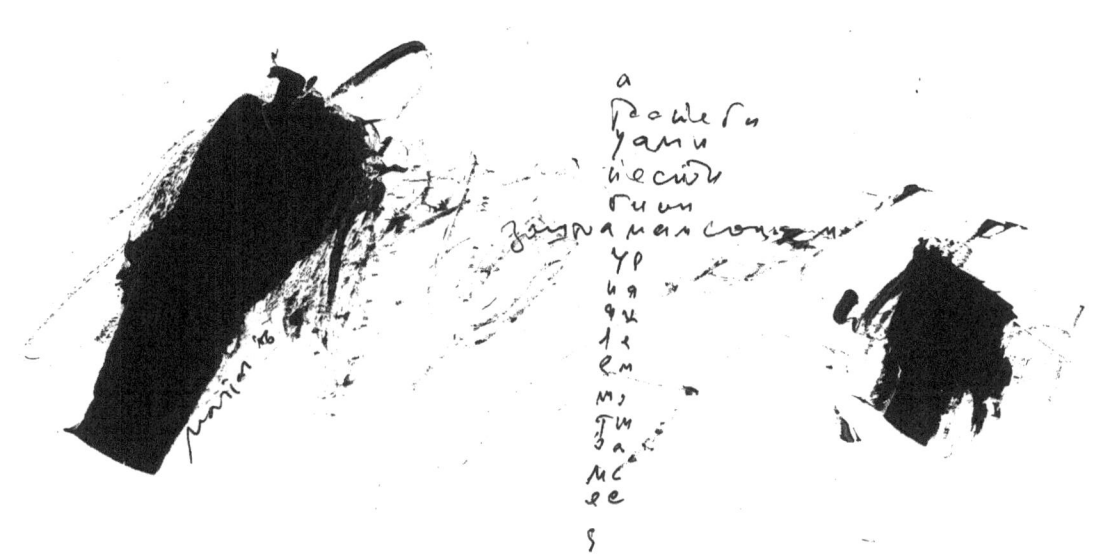

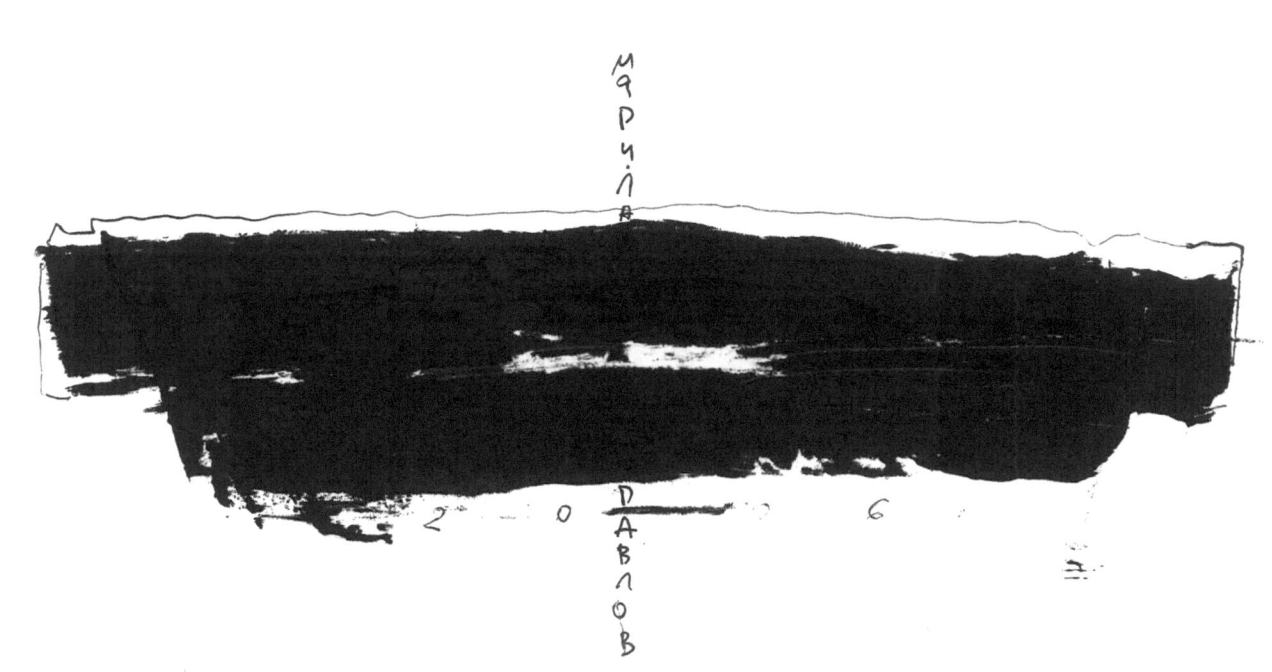

МАРИЛА

2          0          6

ПАВЛОВ

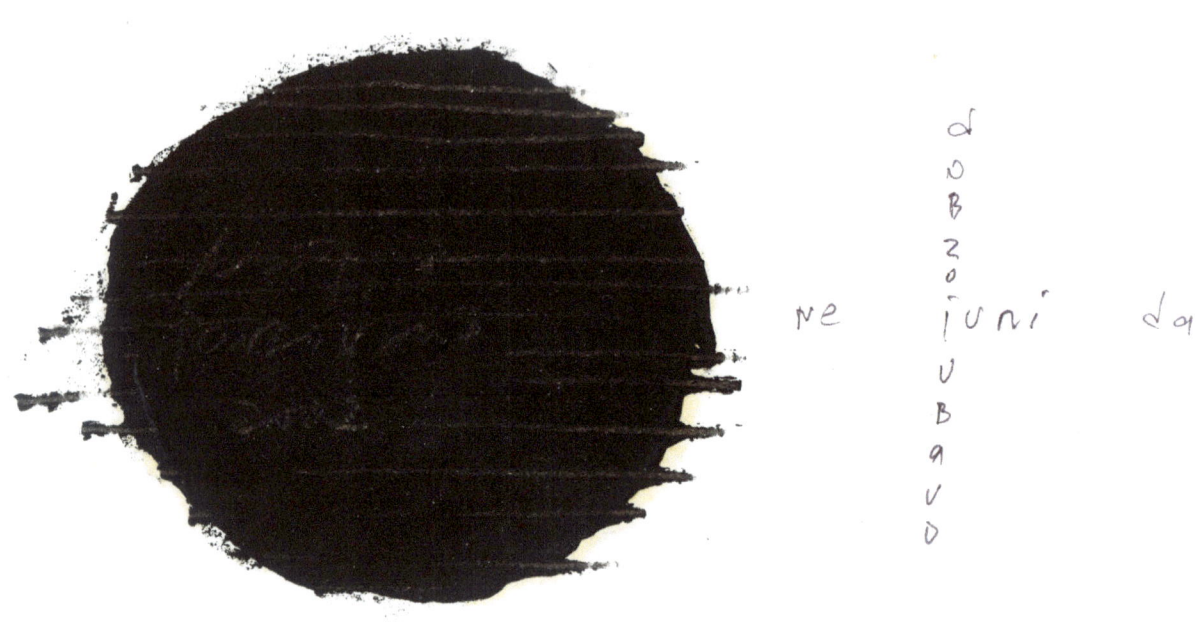

ne  juni  da

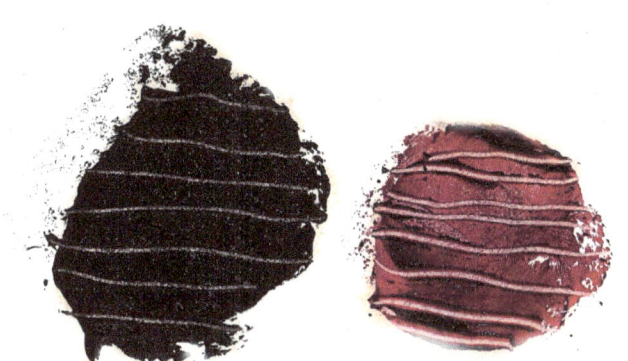

Maria Parvovsus
2007, iuni

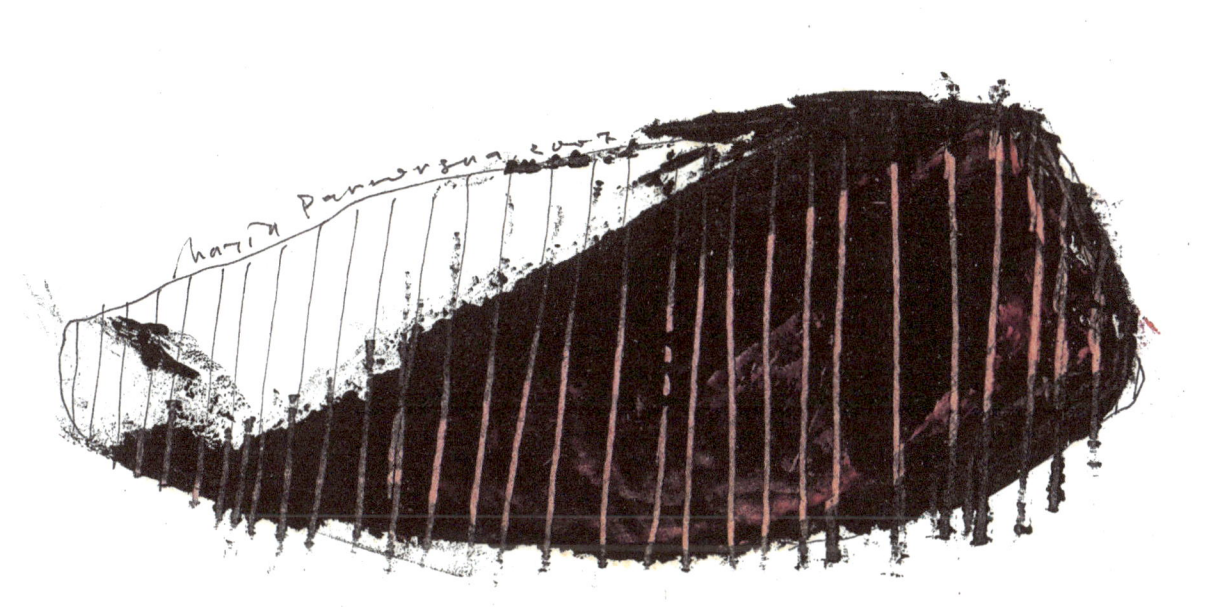

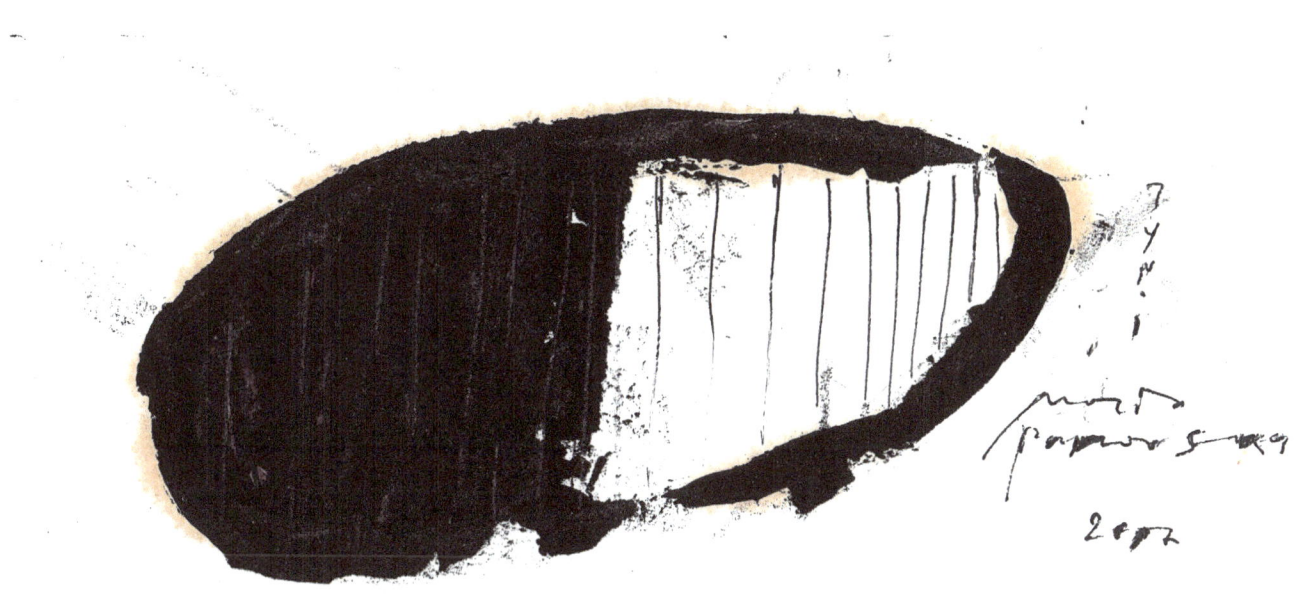

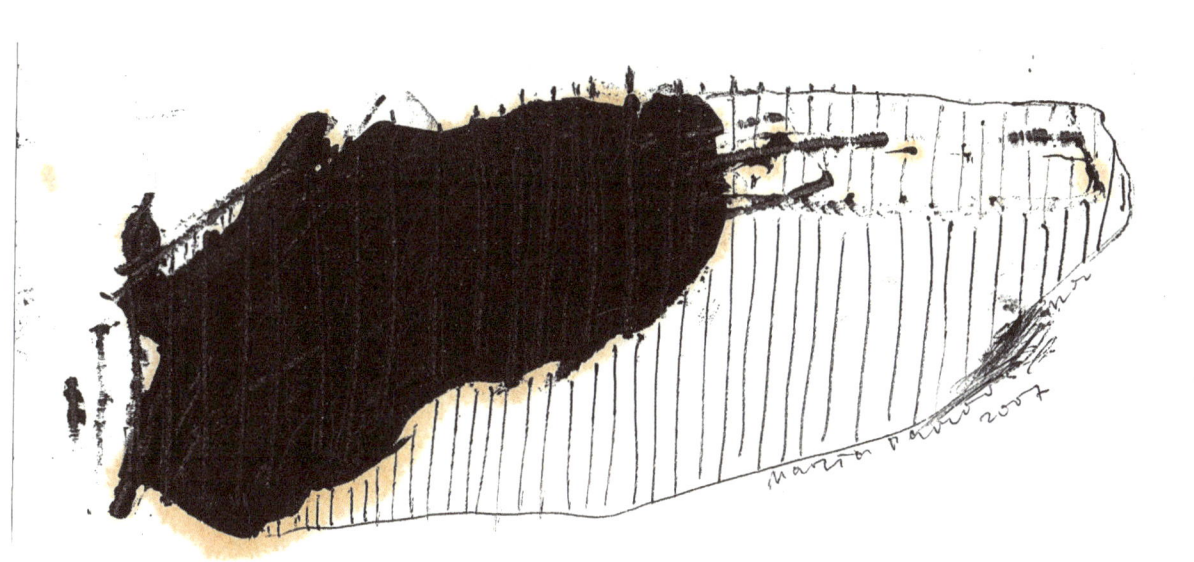

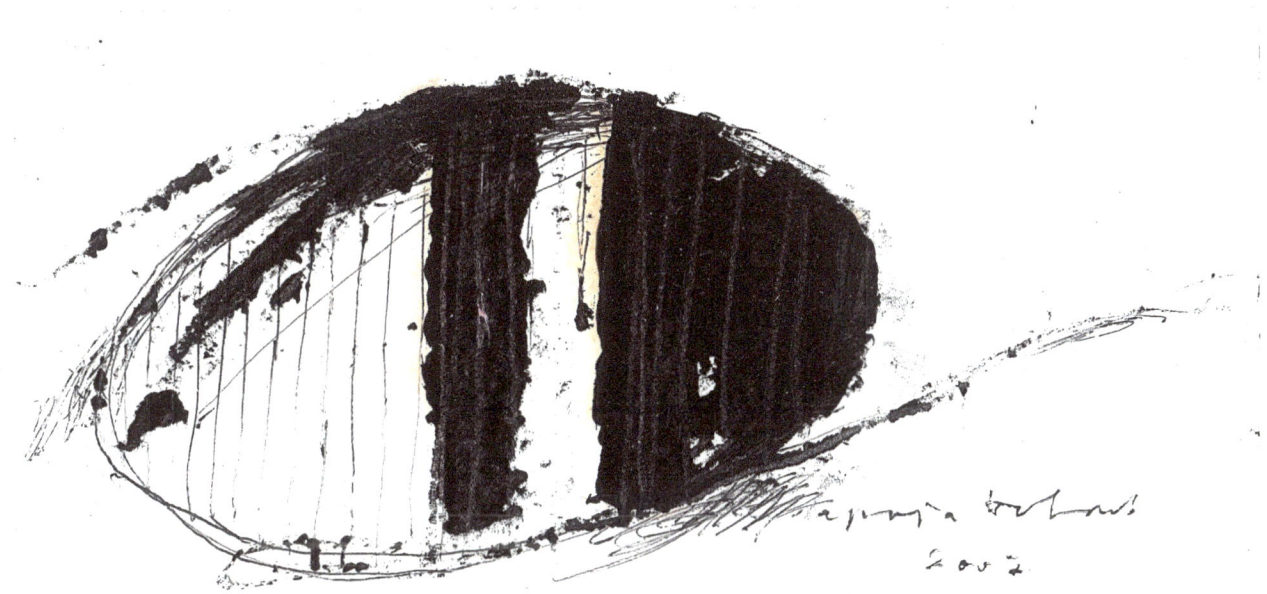

2006 - 2007 red

oil, pen and pencil on cardboard

4 1/2 x 9 3/4 inches each / 11.5 x 24.5 cm

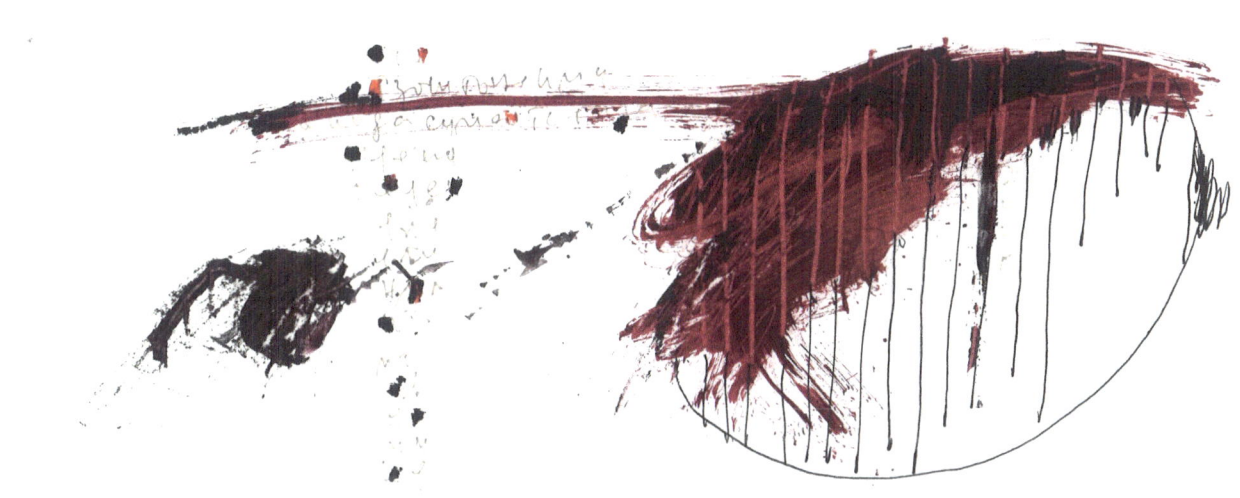

María Parwasuar
2006

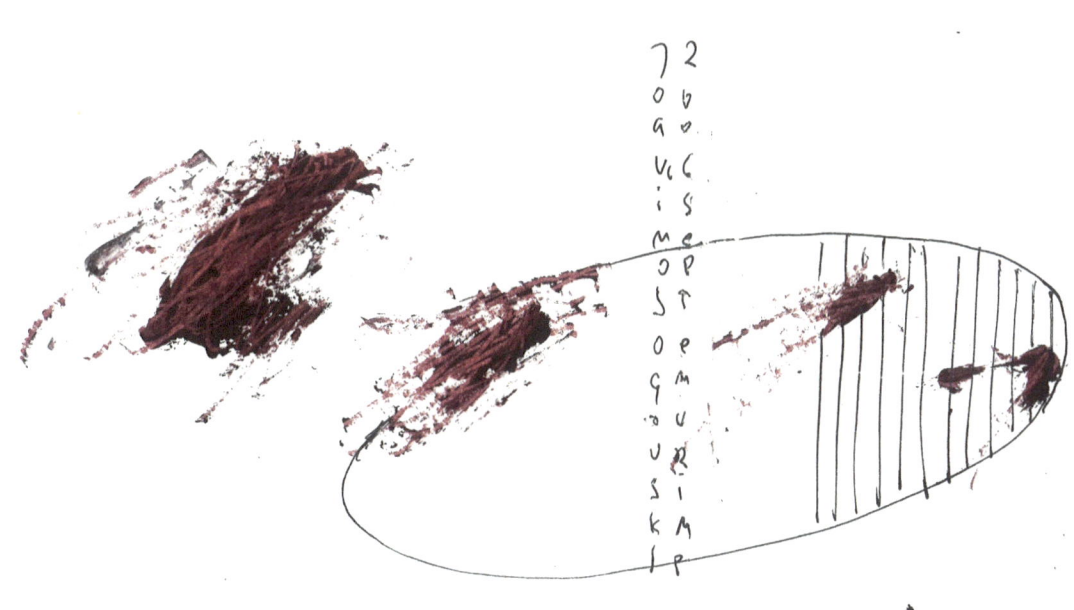

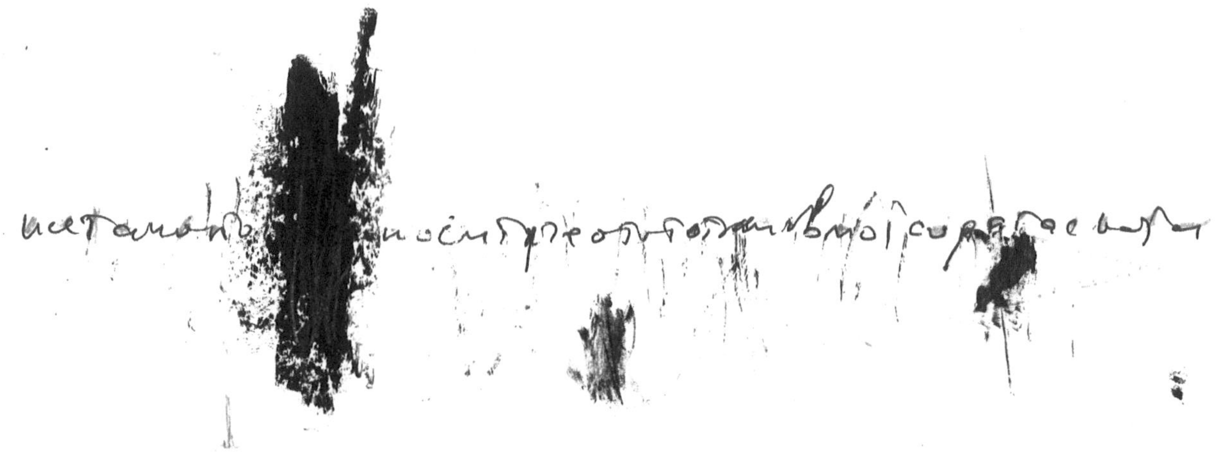

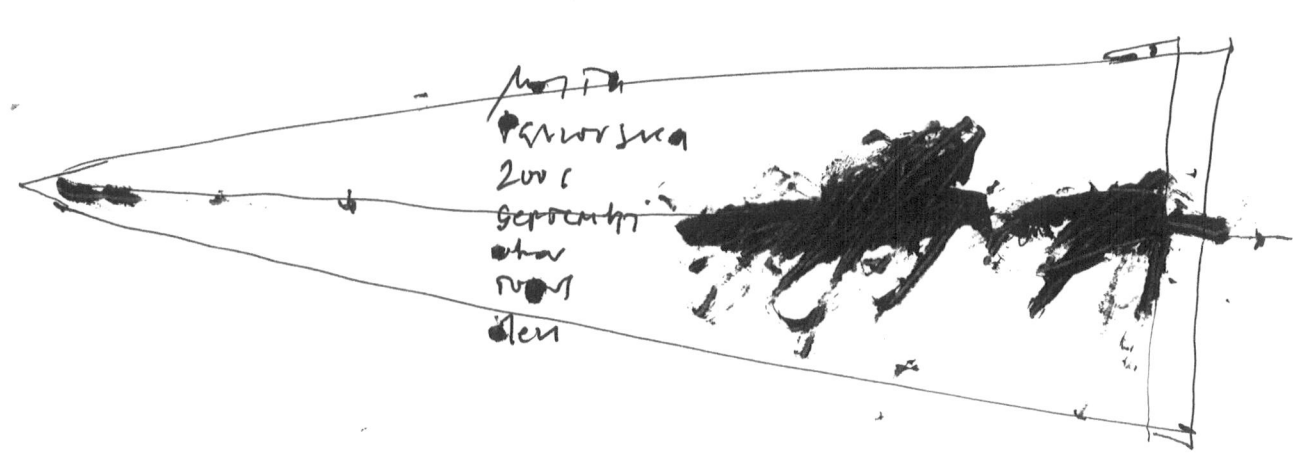

Maria
Pelworska
2006
geroentri
oha
rvon
glen

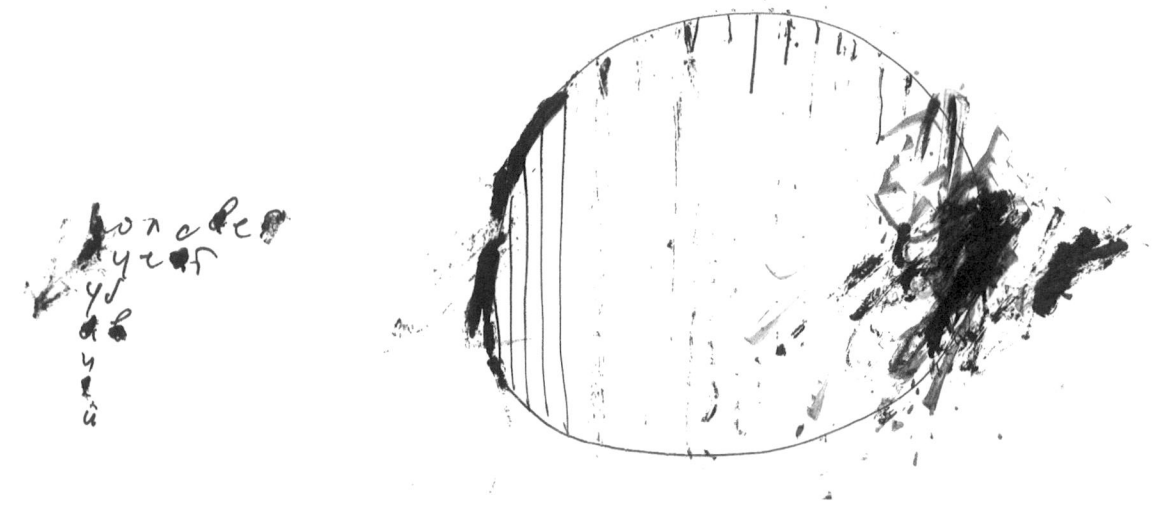

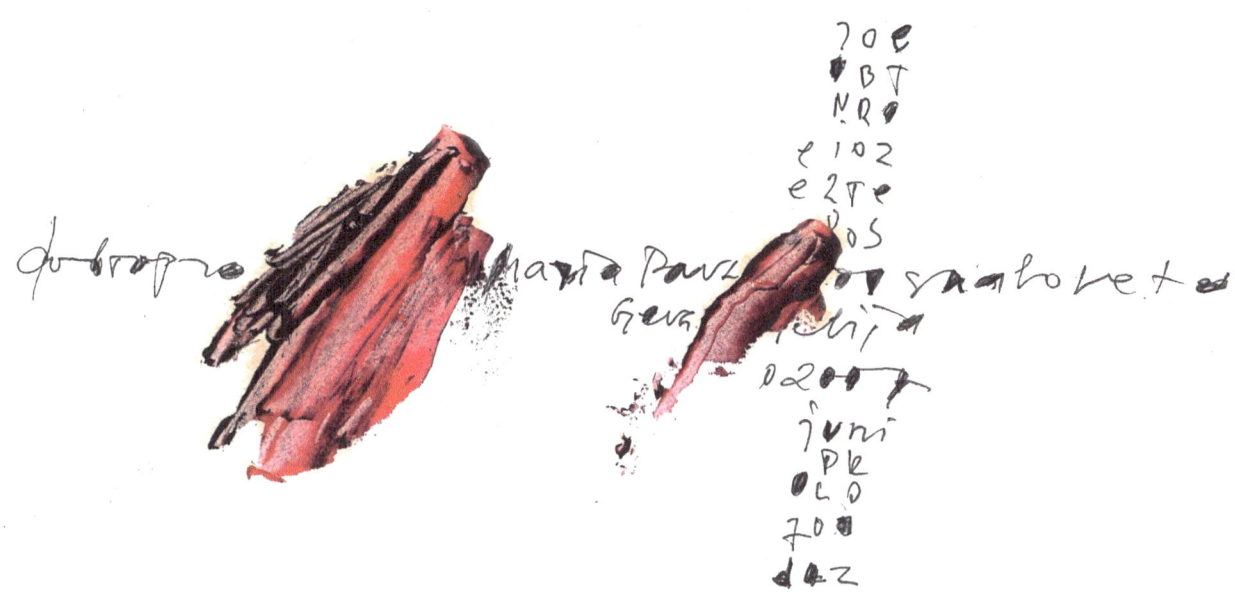

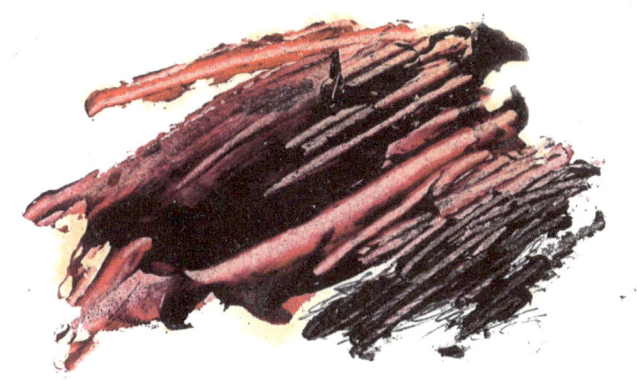

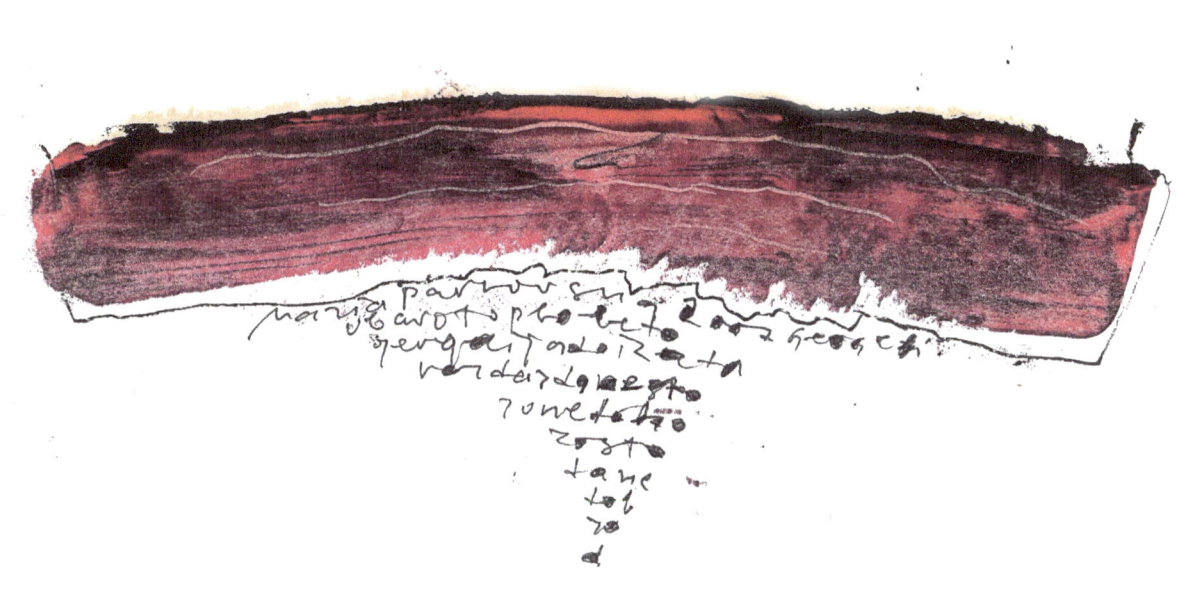

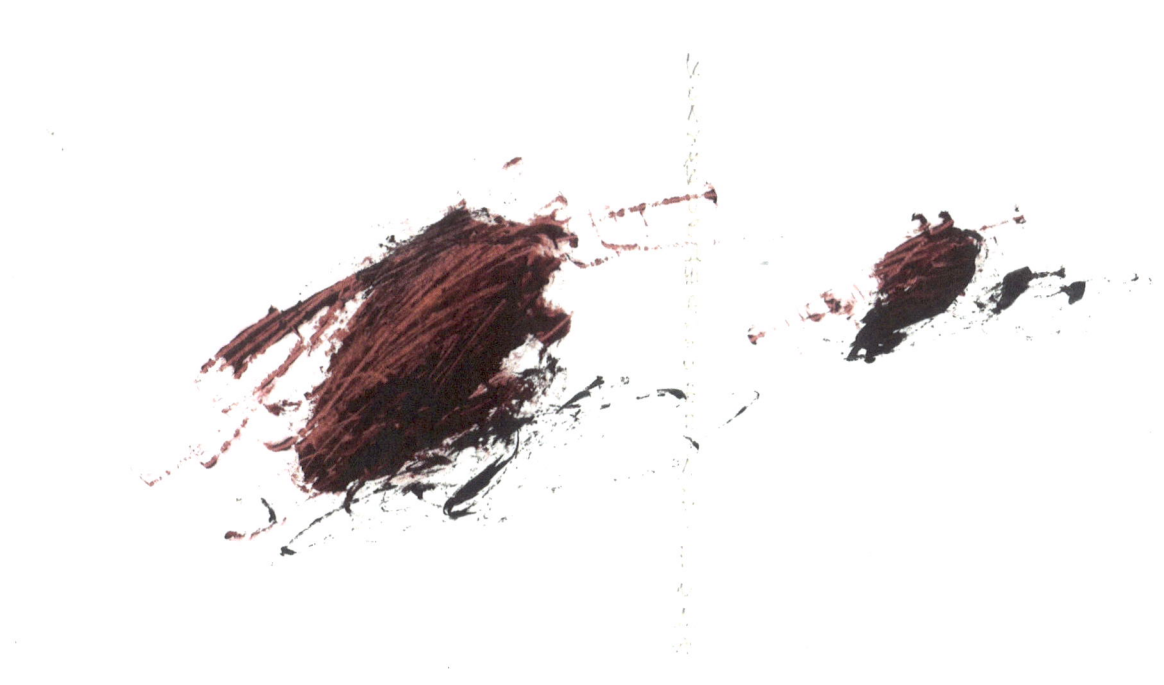

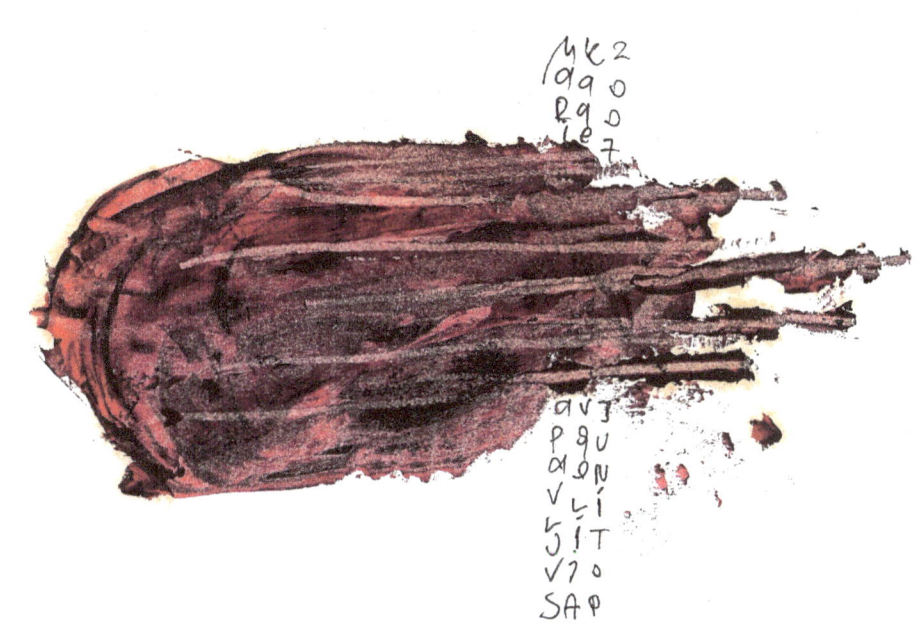

me 2
aa 0
Rg 0
le 7

av j
P a g u
a n i
v l i
5 j T
v 1 0
SA P

## 2008 lyrical

oil, pen and pencil on cardboard

4 1/2 x 9 3/4 inches each / 11.5 x 24.5 cm

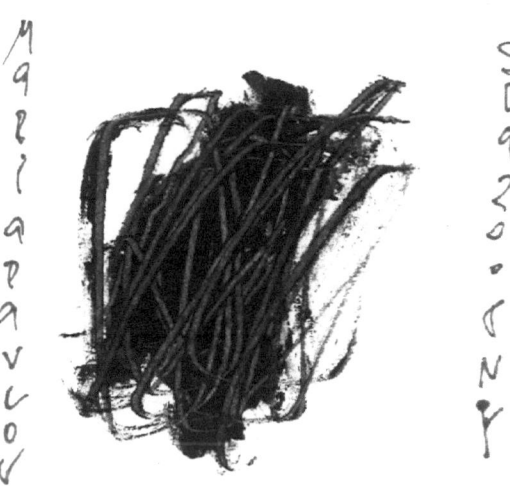

MARIA PAVLOV

SUGAR 30. AUG

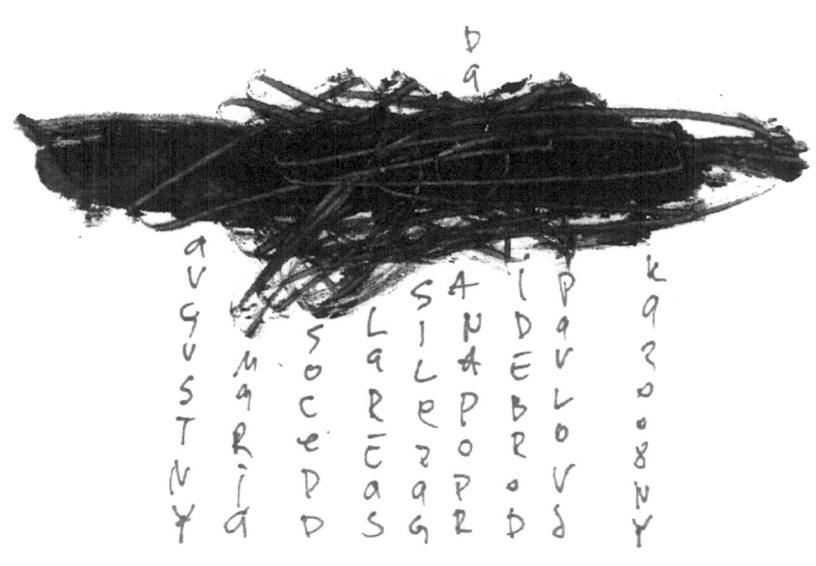

DA9

AUGUSTNY
MARIA
SOCEDD
LAREAS
SILERAG
ANAPOPR
IDEBROD
PAVLOVS
k93008NY

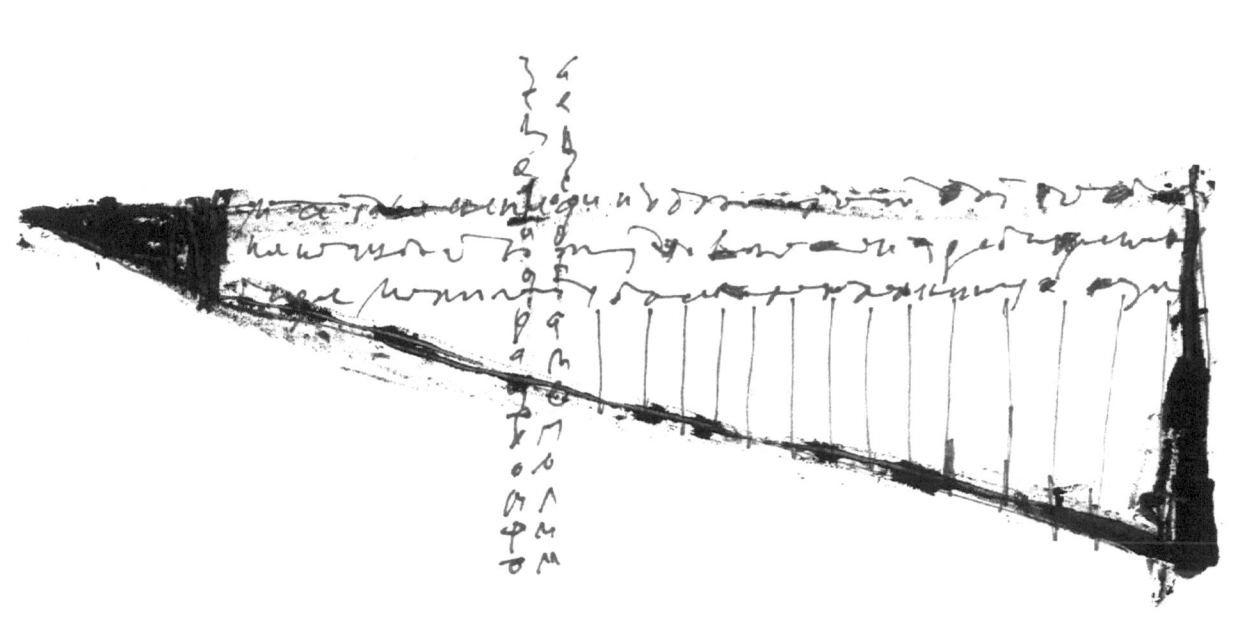

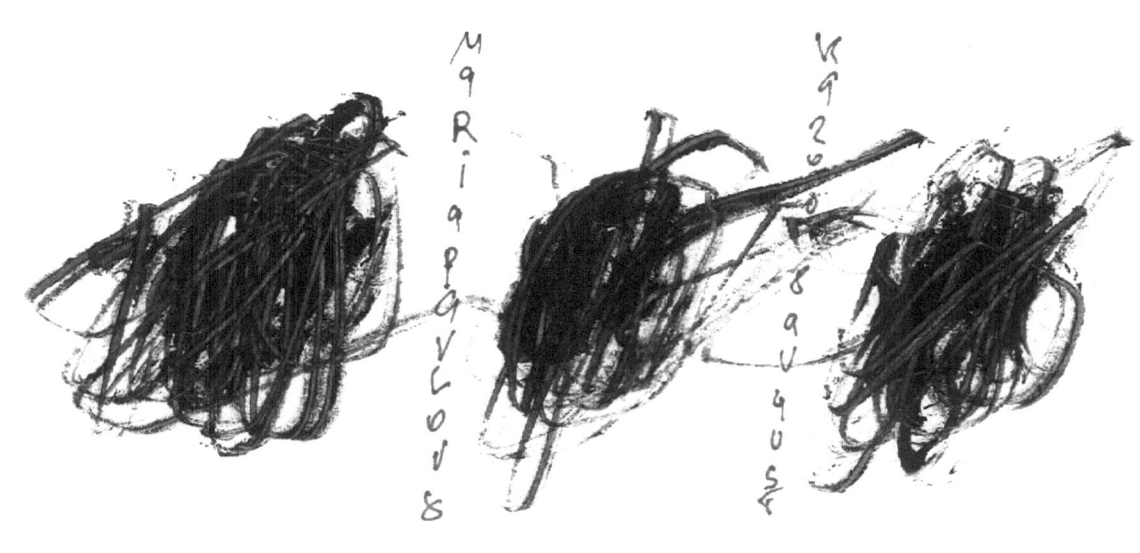

Maria
New York
2008
august

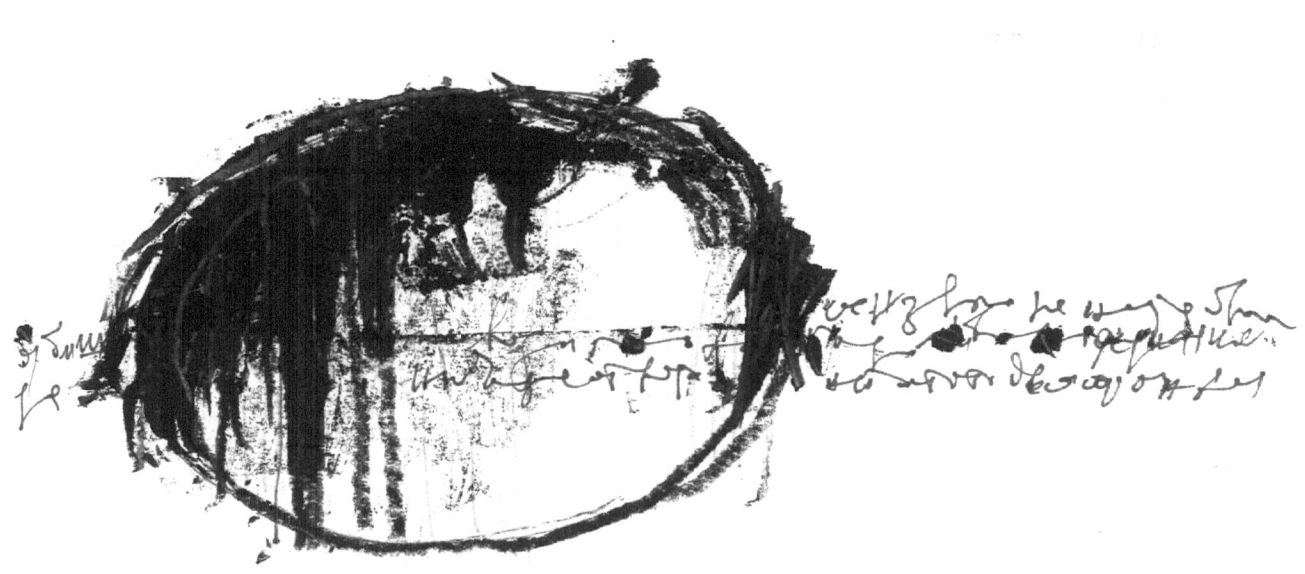

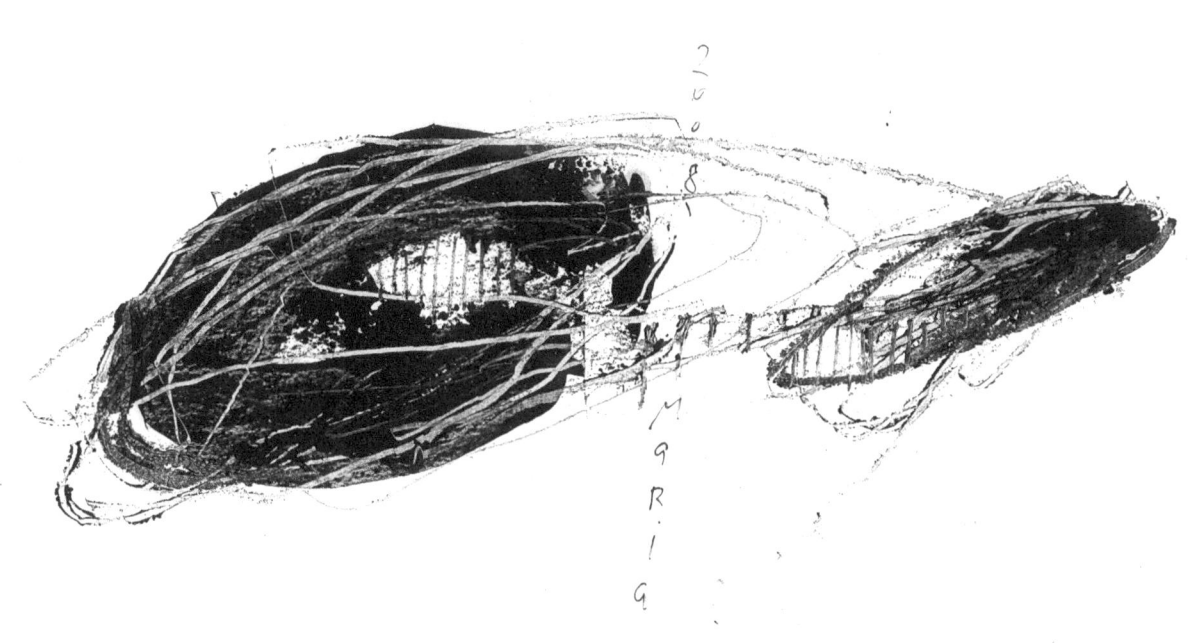

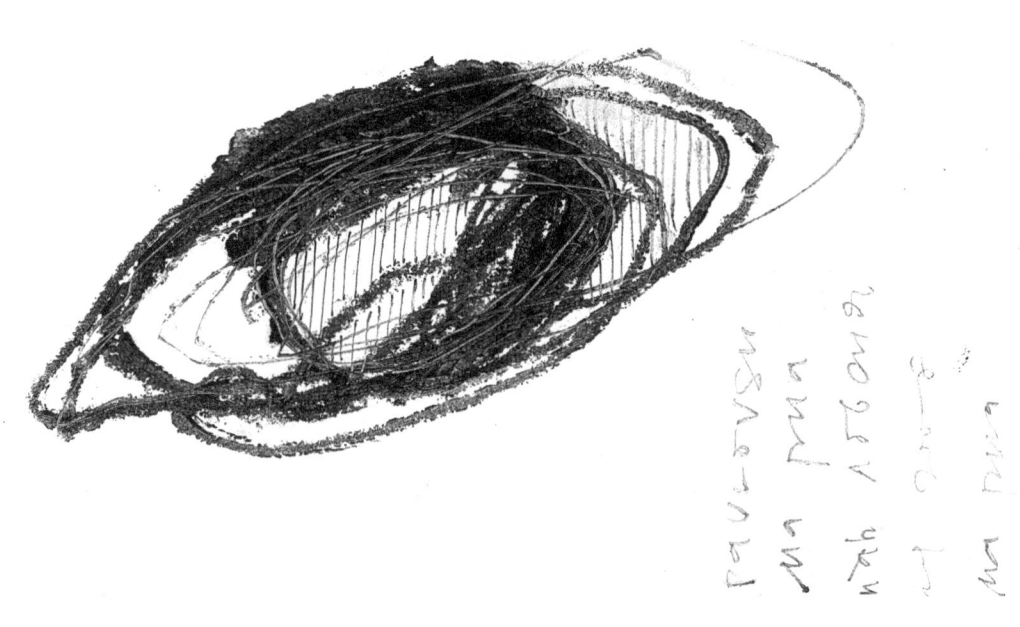

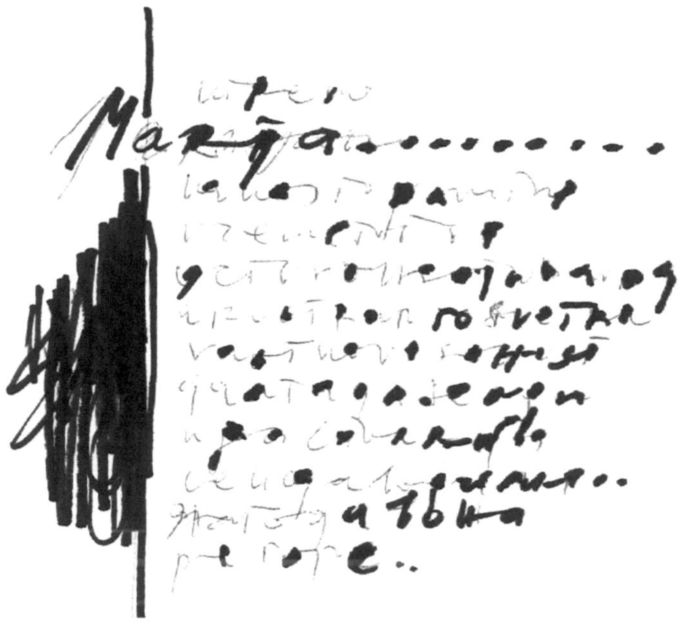

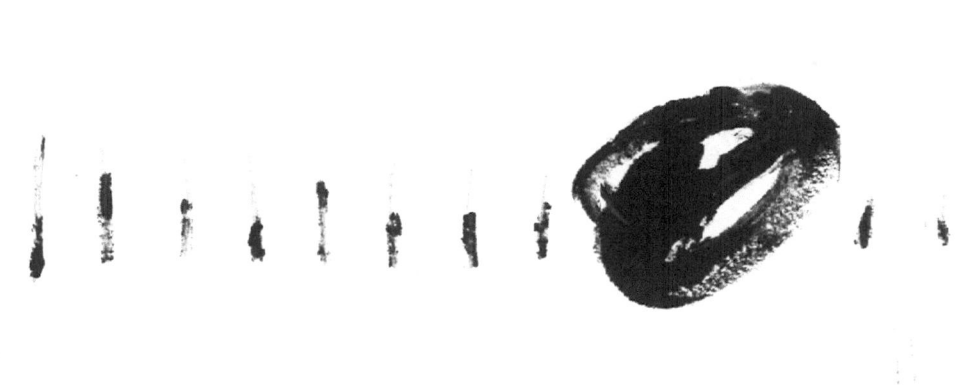

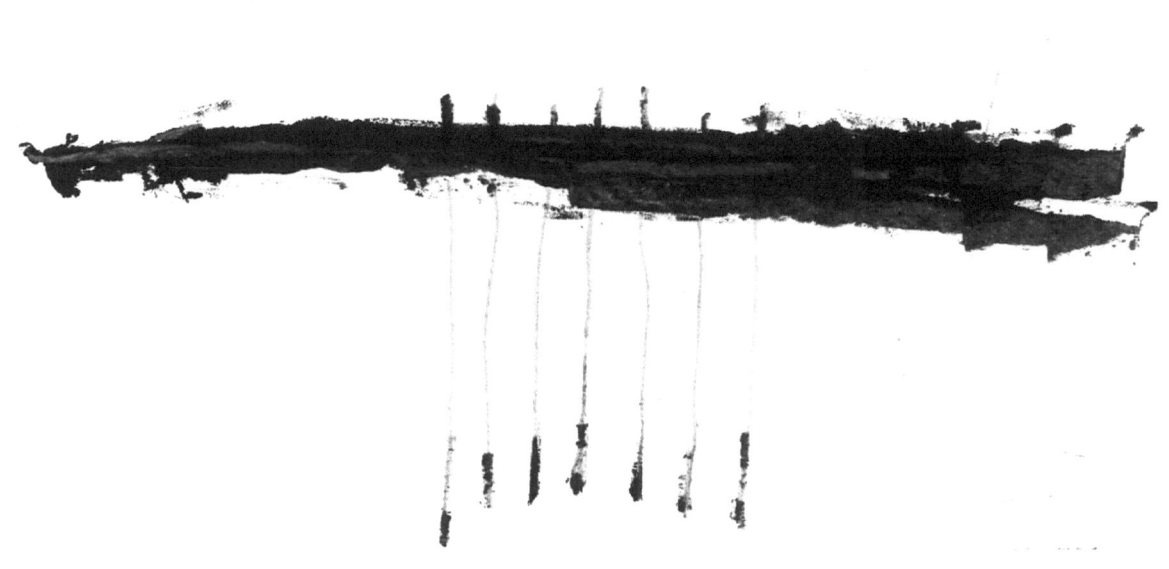

2013 - 2014  diaries

oil, oil stick, and pencil on paper

9 x 11 3/4 inches each / 23 x 30 cm

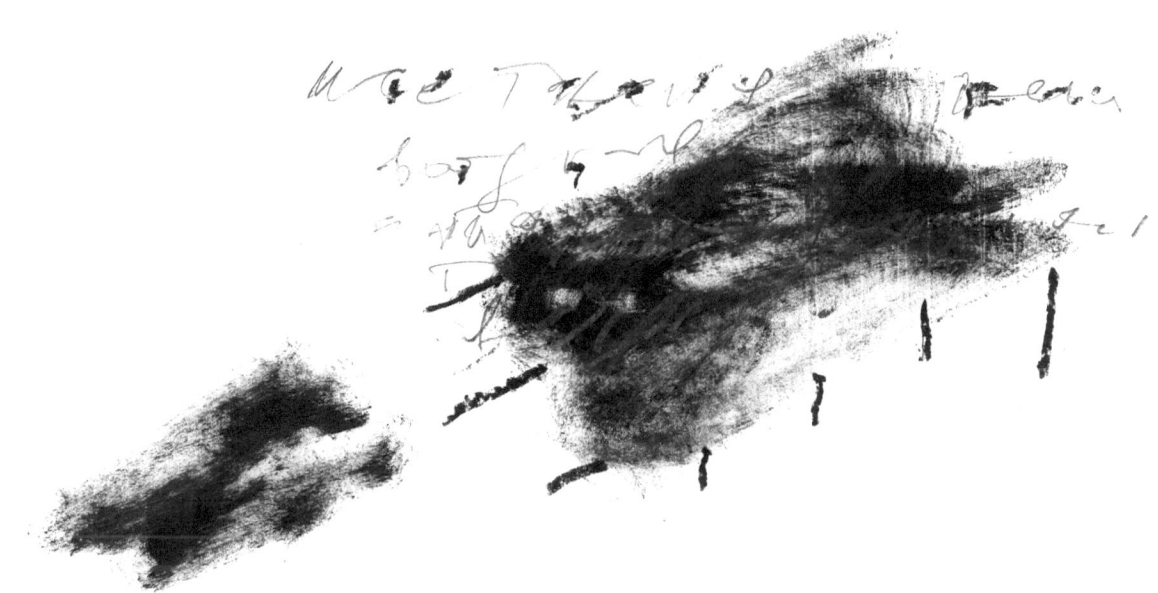

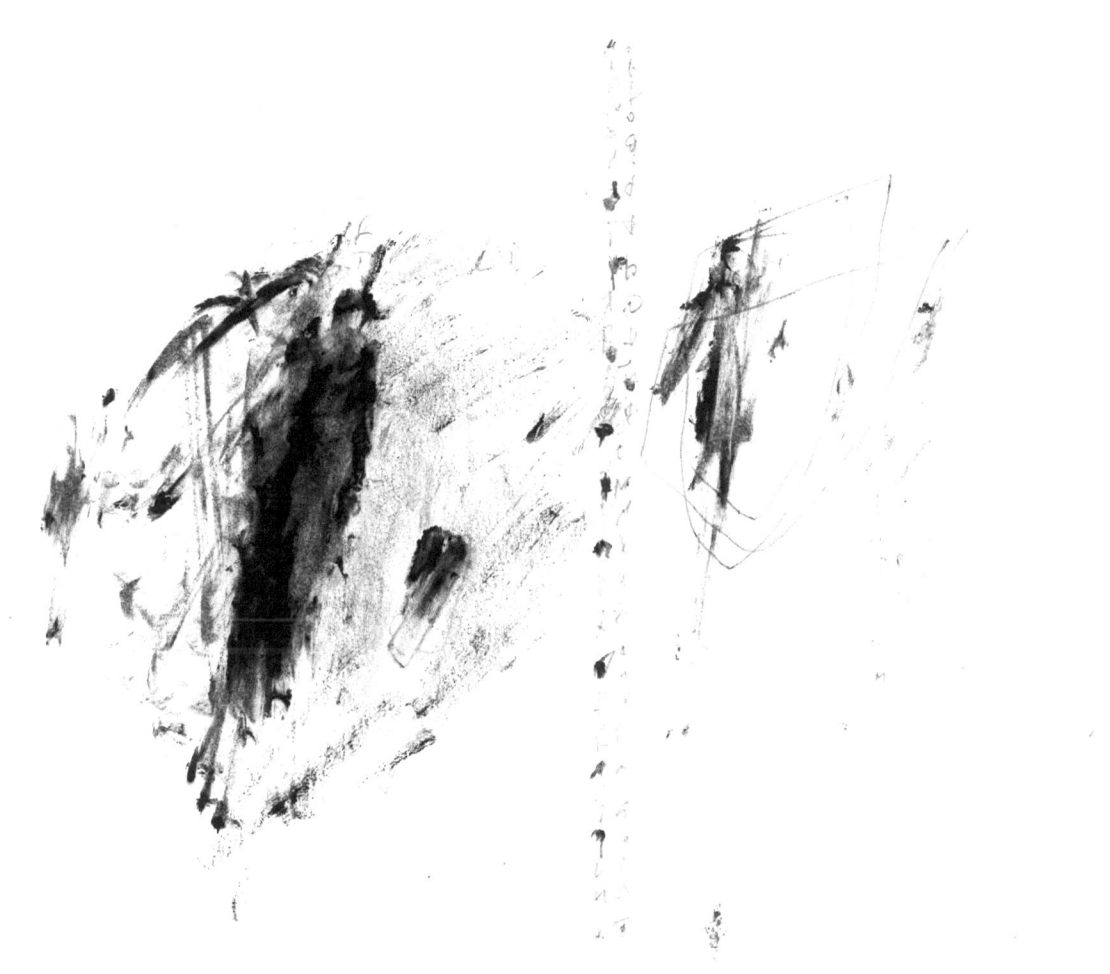

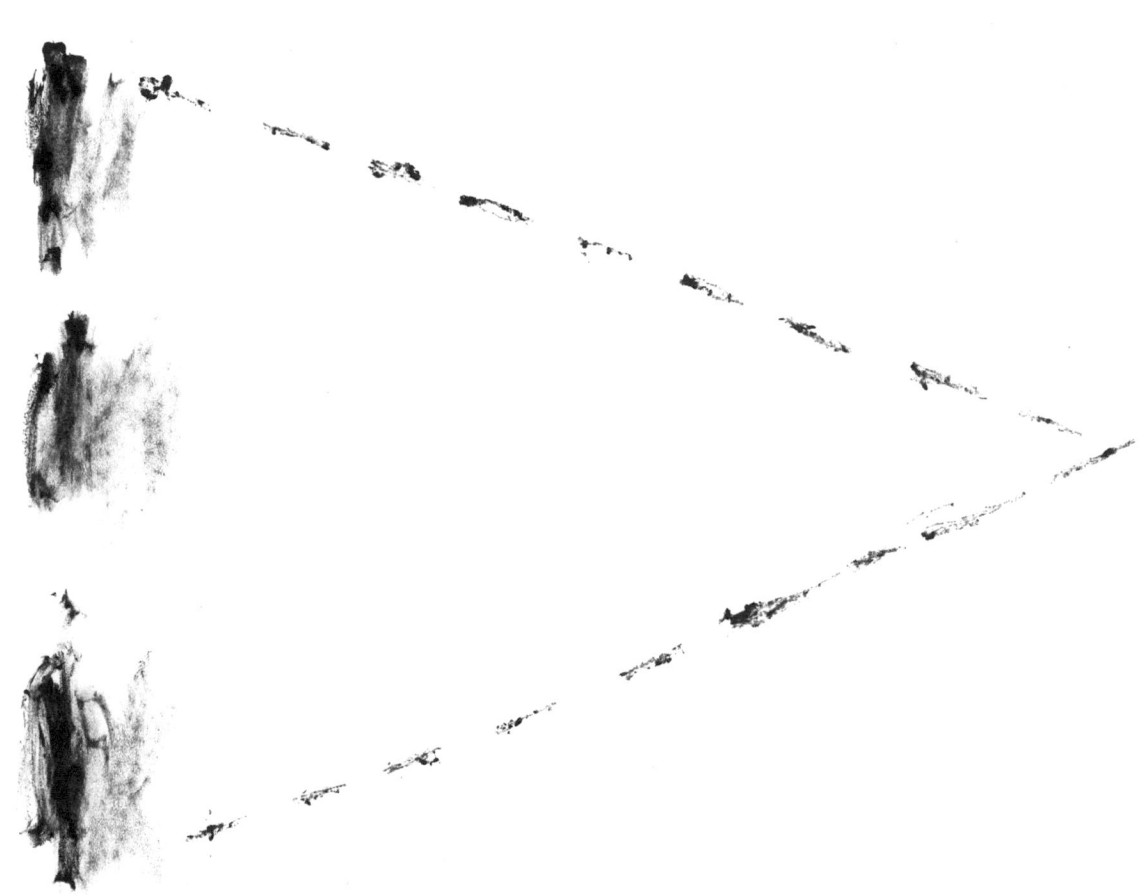

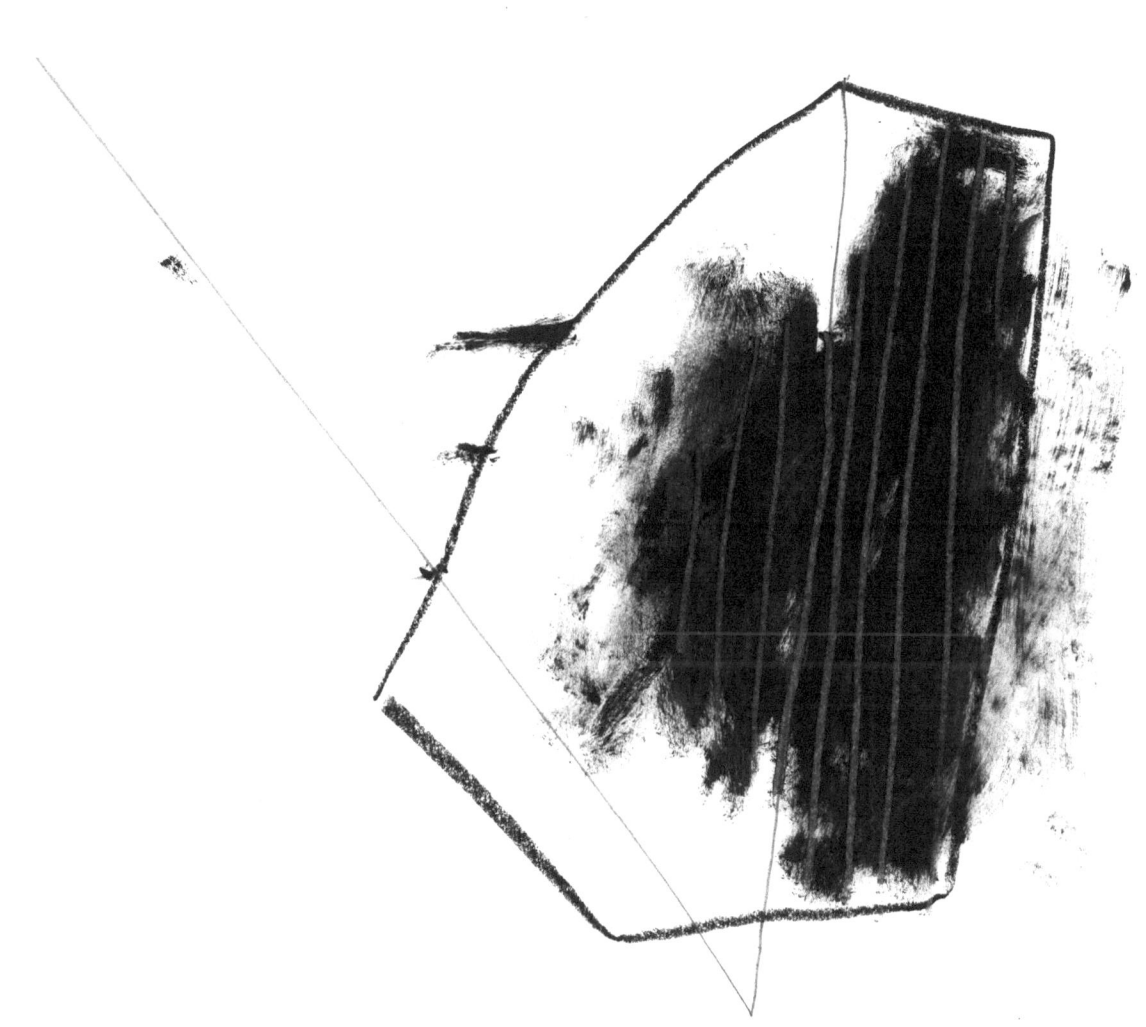

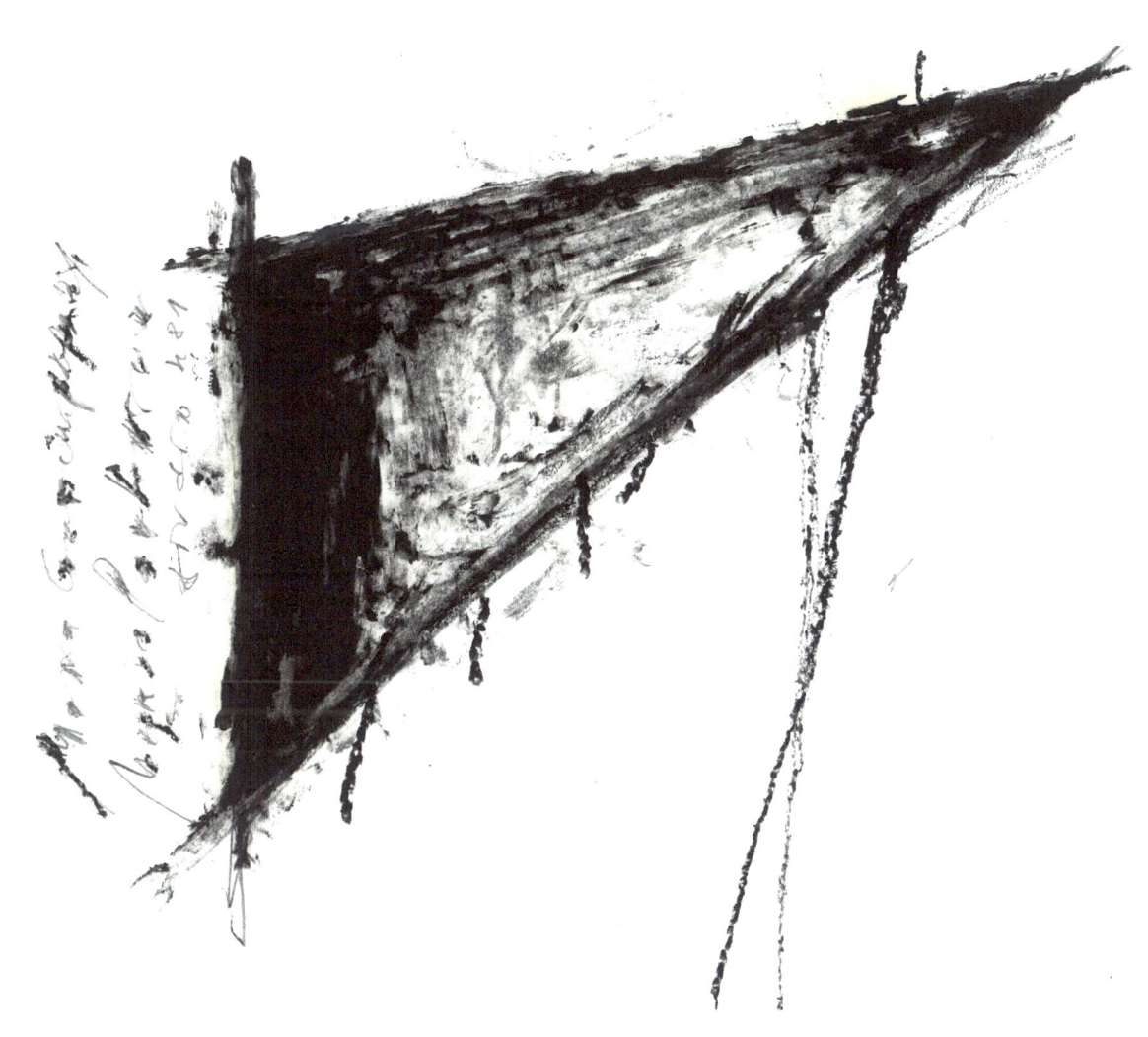

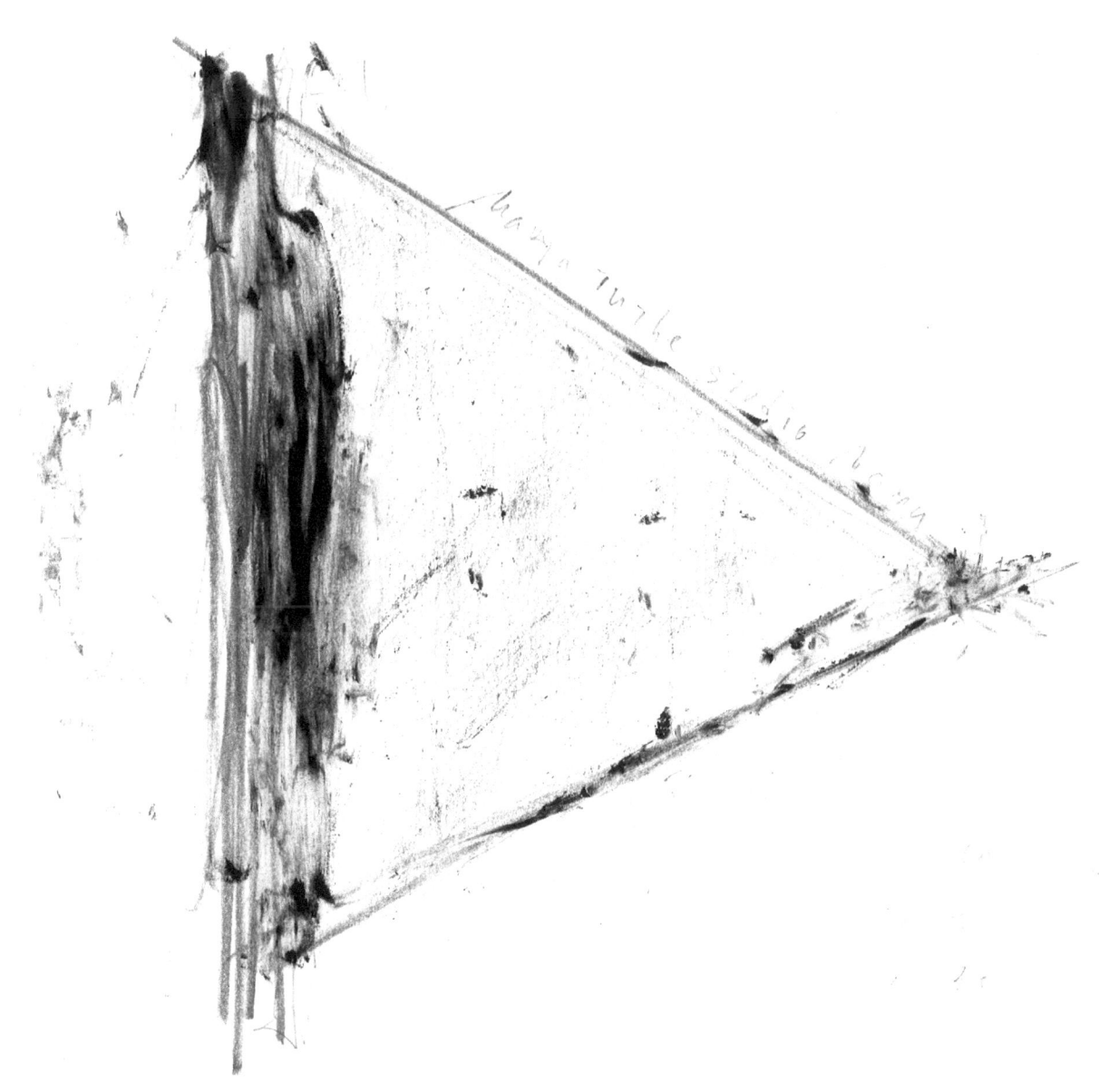

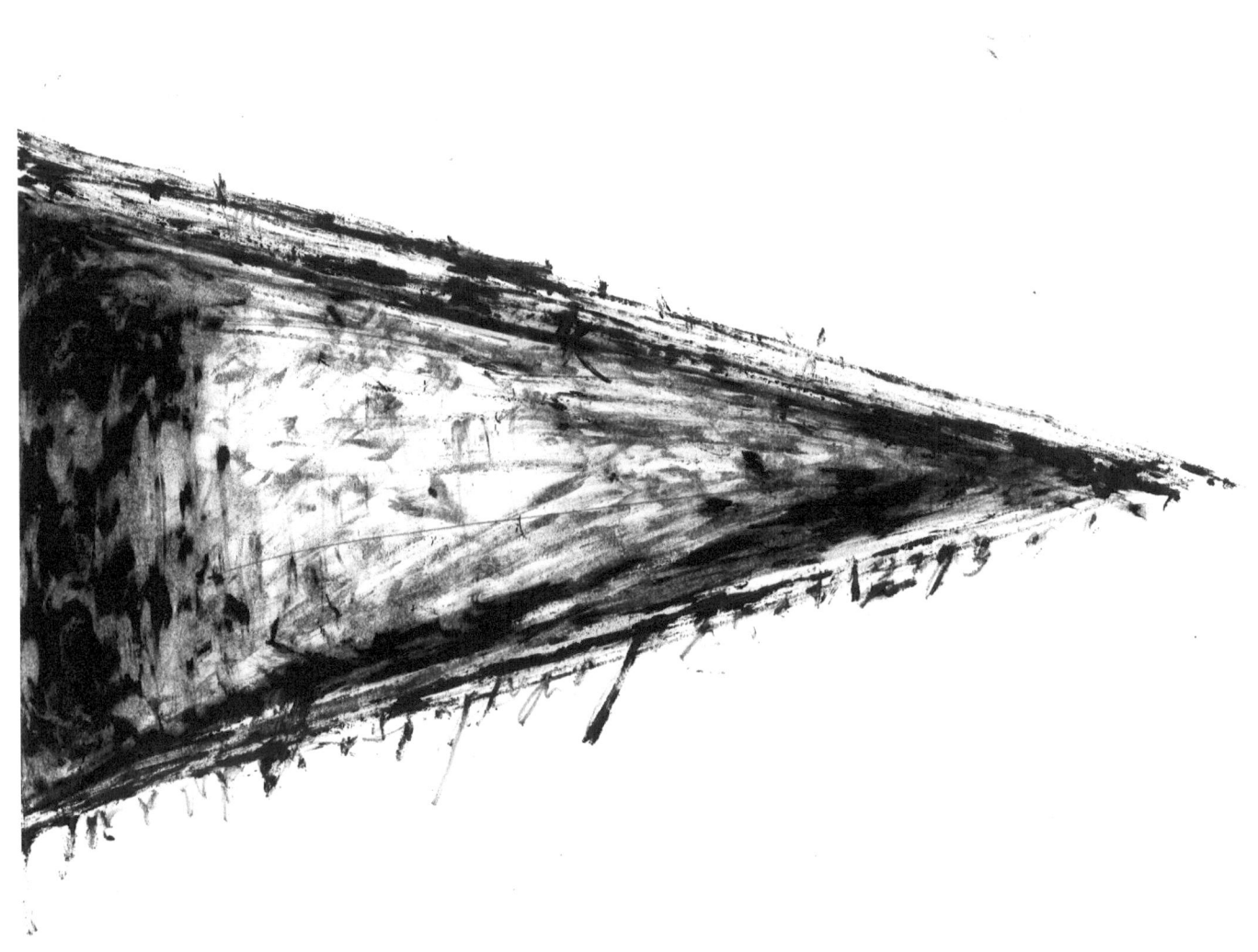

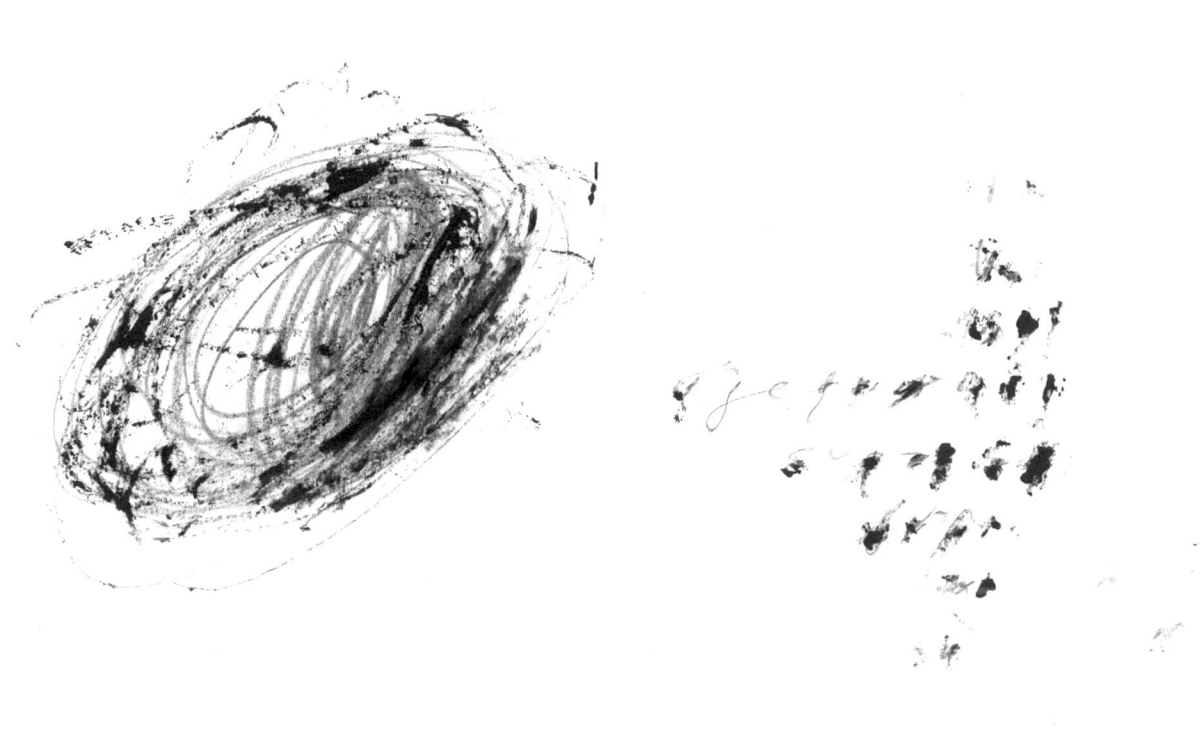

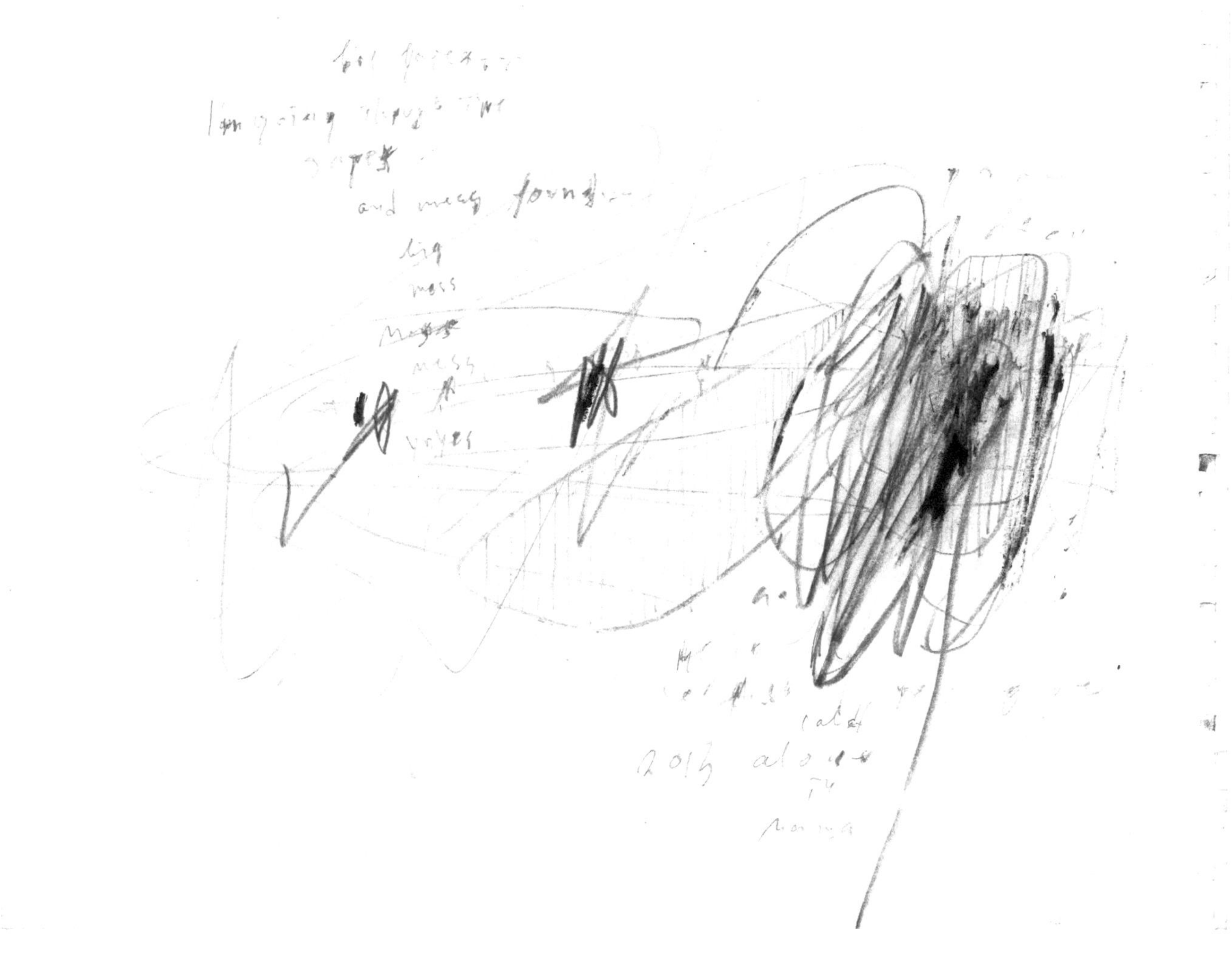
and mess found
big
mess
mess

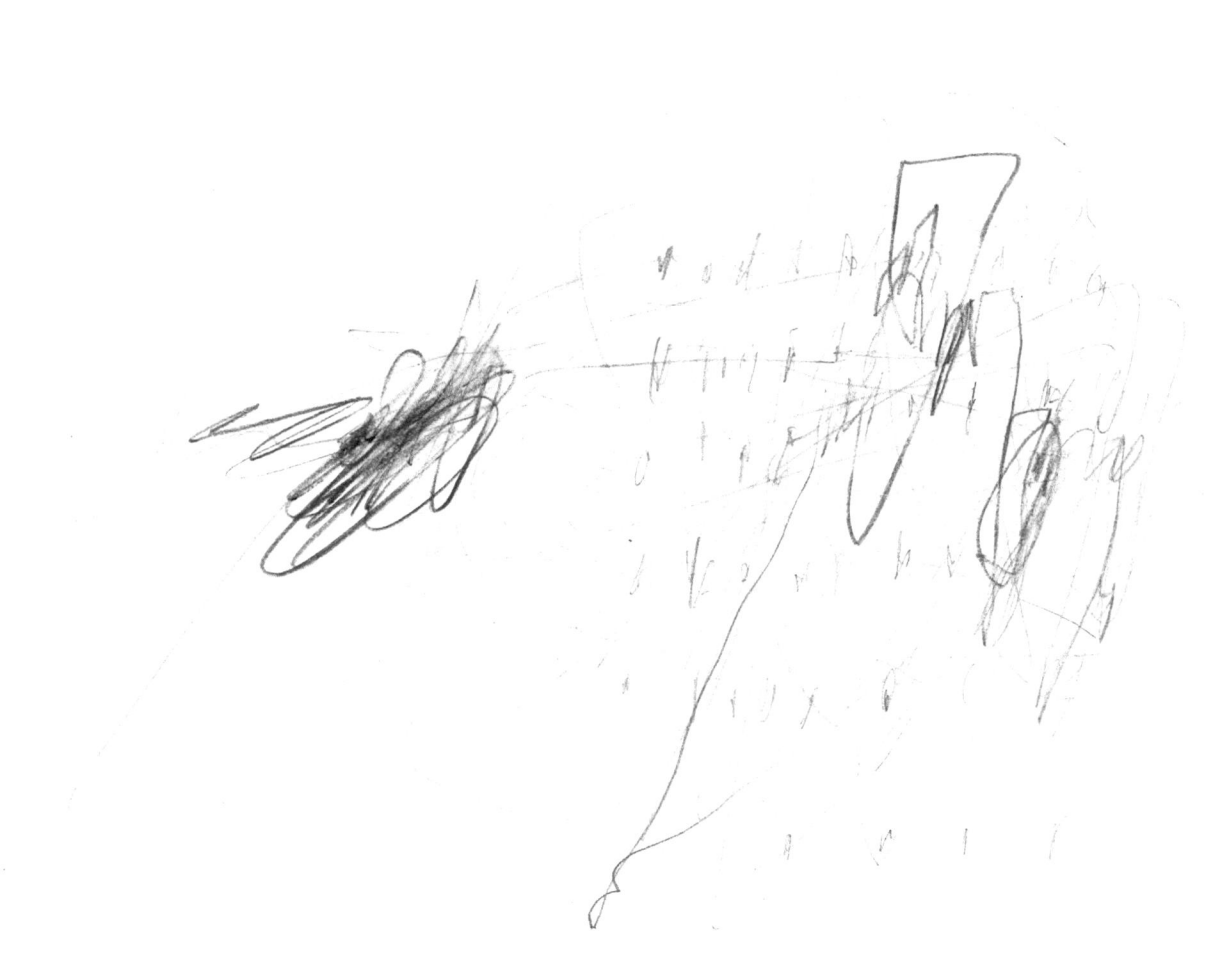

2013.
9:40pm

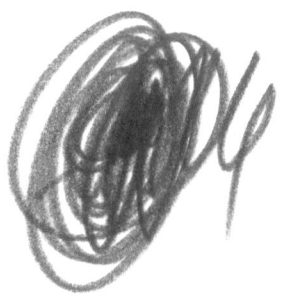

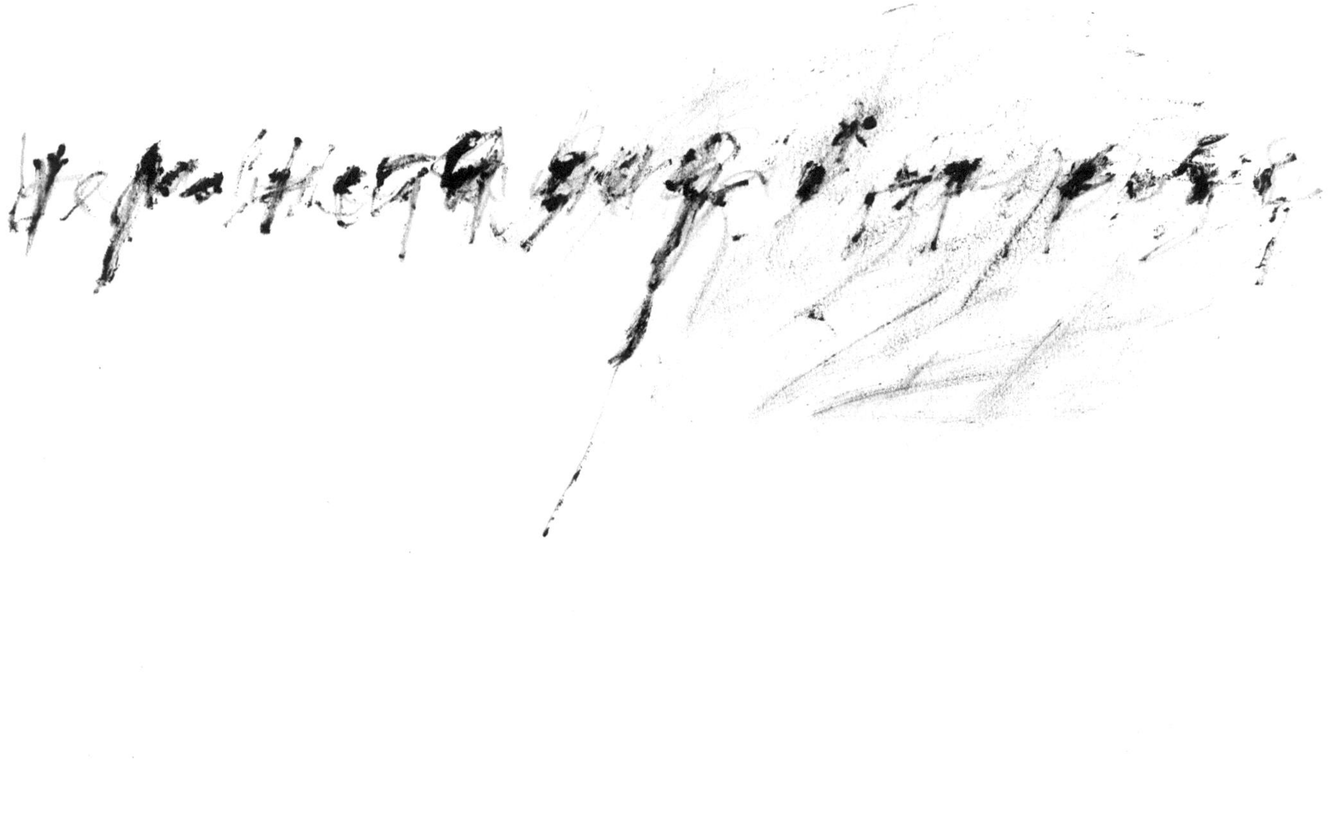

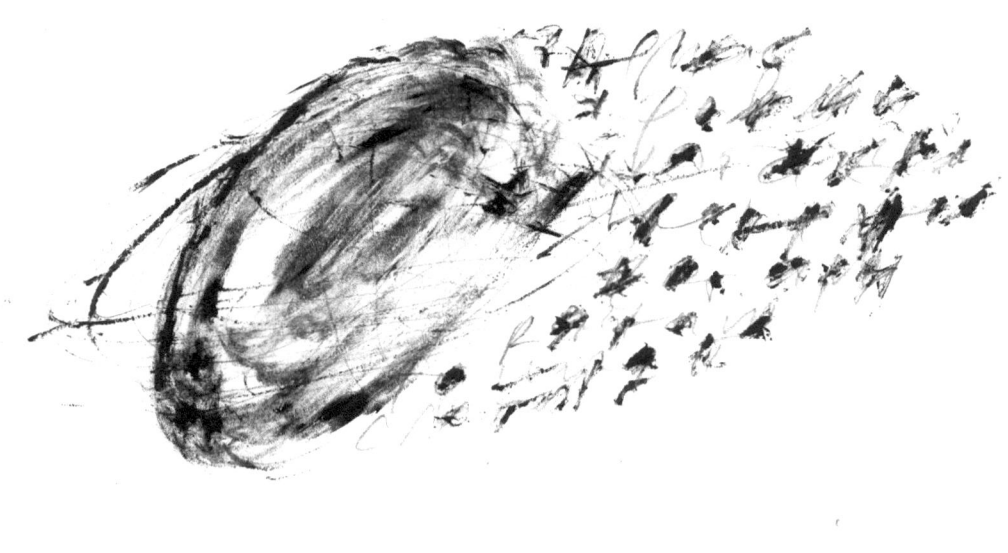

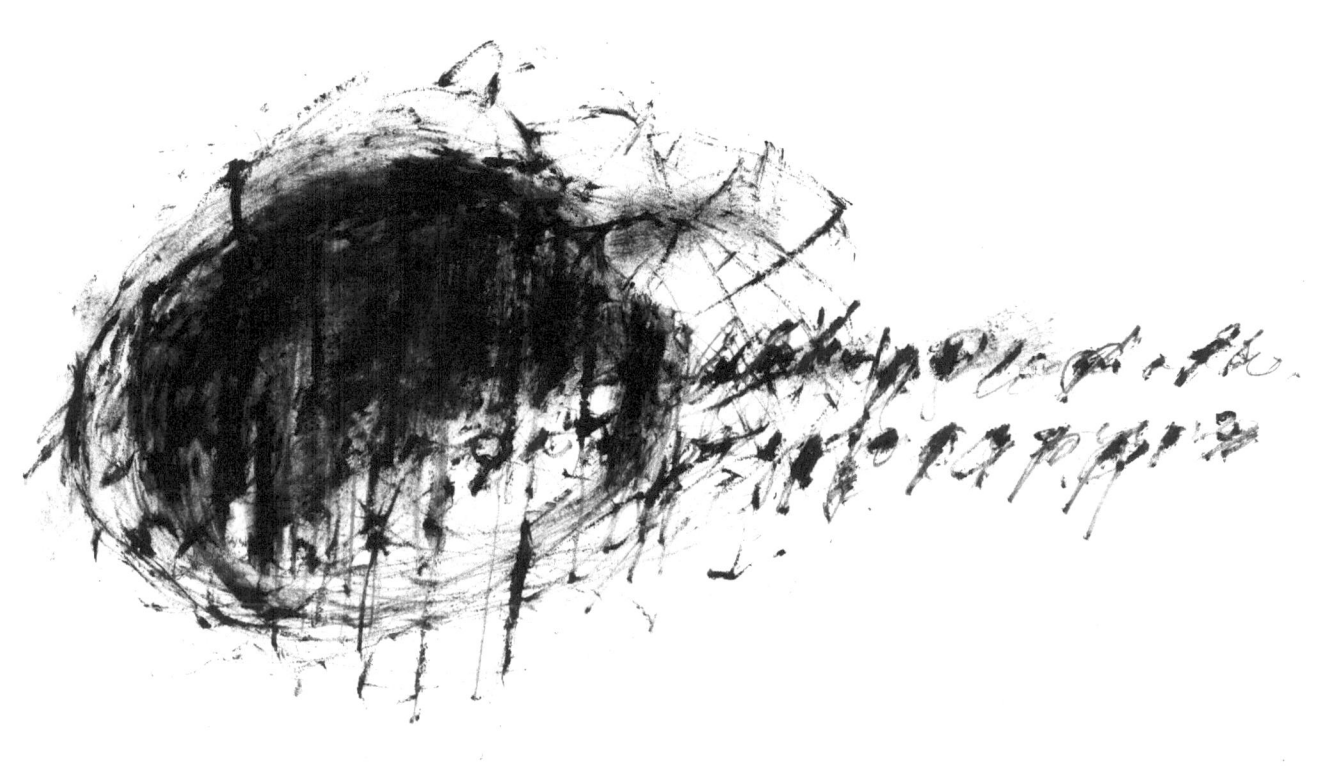

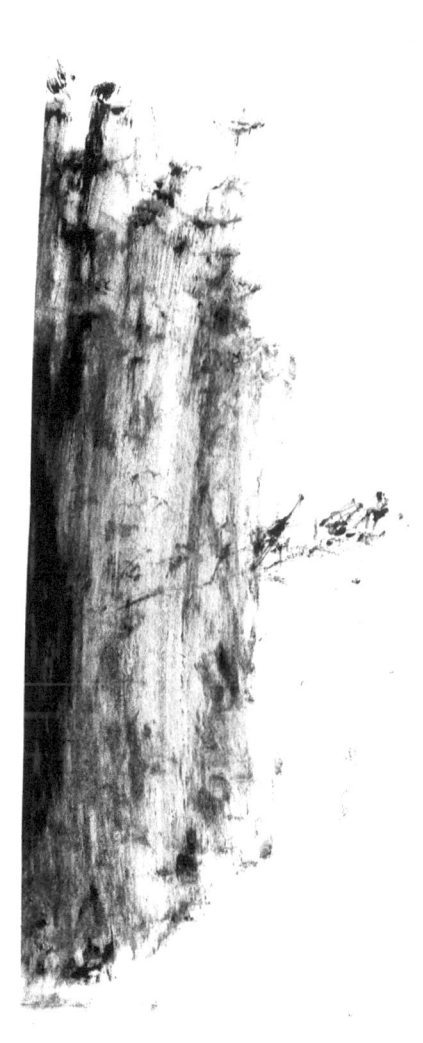

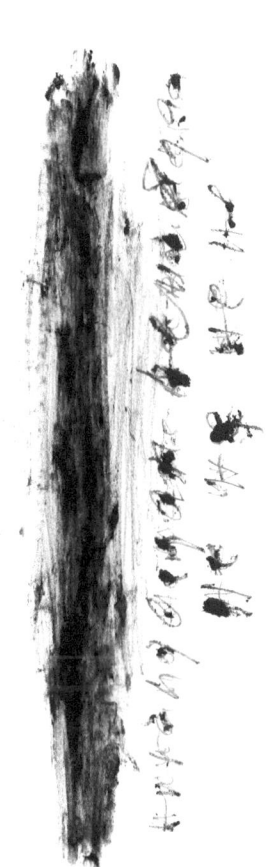

2014 - 2015  equation

oil, oil stick, and pencil on paper

4 1/2 x 4 inches each / 11.5 x 10 cm

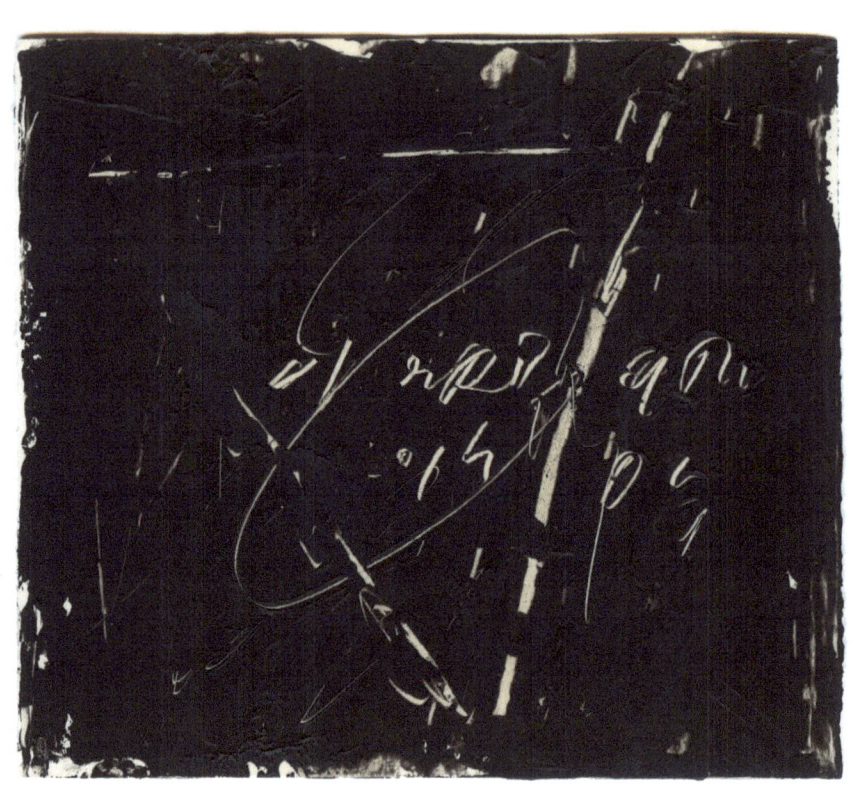

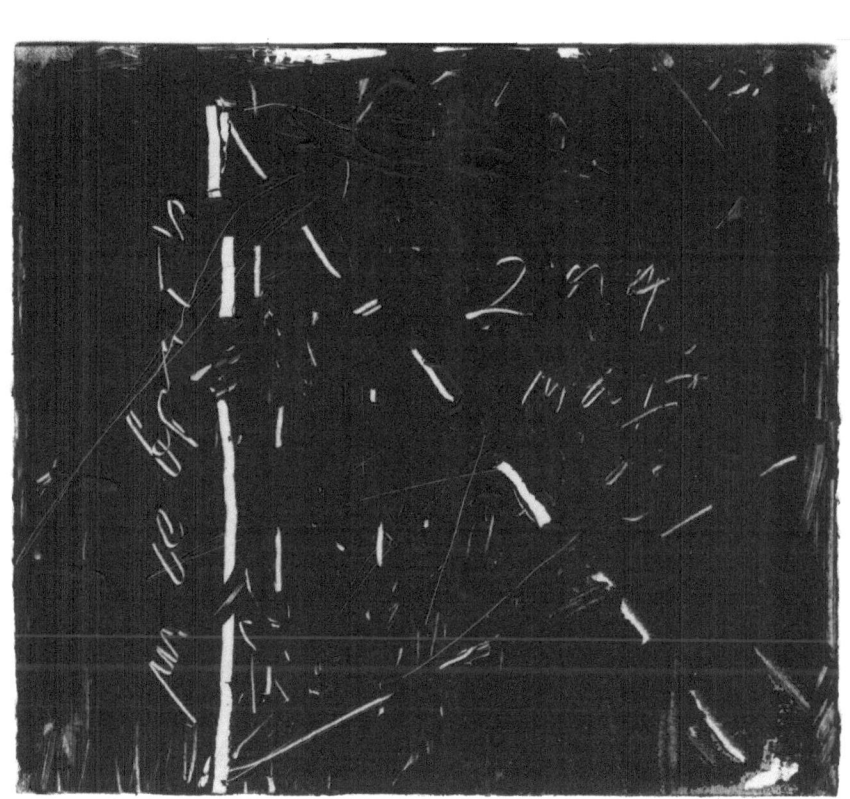

## About the Artist

Maria Pavlovska was born in Skopje, Macedonia (Former Yugoslavia) in 1975.     Her work has been featured around the globe in over 28 solo shows and more than 100 group international exhibitions including Art Basel Miami, The Kunsthalle-Vienna and Kunsthalle-Krems (Austria), Gallery Lang (Vienna), Cite Internationale des Arts, The Dock (Paris), Museum of Contemporary Art, The National Gallery, Museum of the City - Skopje (Macedonia), City House in Nurnberg (Germany), Station Gallery, Gallery MC, The Open Space Gallery, Citibank (New York), FLA Gallery (Connecticut), Viota Gallery (San Juan - Puerto Rico), Prima Center (Berlin), MANA Contemporary and Drawing Rooms (New Jersey). Her work is held in private and public collections worldwide, including embassies, museums, galleries and libraries.

Her artistic journey started at an early age, she was noticed as one of Balkan - Europe's promising young talents. She took up residencies in Paris, Vienna and Nuremberg (Germany). After her first solo in New York in 2007, she has lived and continued to be active in the New York art scene. Her artwork has been featured in  many magazines, newspaper articles, and museum and gallery catalogs world-wide.  She was runner-up for the Venice Biennale in 2015. Her project "A Reaction" was nominated to represent her country, Macedonia for that year. Maria participated in Art Basel Miami in 2014, , represented by MANA, was awarded Citibank Artist of the Year - an Annual Solo Show at the 60th St/5th Ave. branch in 2011, and has been awarded 11 Arts grants throughout her career. Her studio residence has been at MANA Contemporary, a leading Contemporary Art Center in the New York City area since 2012..

Hailing from a family of creative artists - her father is an esteemed painter internationally, (National Order of Merit Award for the Arts 2011, Macedonia) , her older sister is a leading musicologist and her younger sister is an international classical pianist - it is apparent that her artistic energy is ingrained within the very fabric of her being. Although part of a distinguished cultural family legacy, Maria has achieved significant recognition in her own right.

Critics have described her work as having "a strong personality" which "translates her topics of choice into pictorial language that demonstrates a quietly powerful eloquence". She has received praise from critics worldwide for her drawings and paintings with work that reflects painting as a battlefield, where light and darkness fight and the result is unpredictable. One sees the lightning bolts of ideas at work, as they are being worked out. This sort of simultaneous image "process / result " dialectic lies frozen in space, stimulating the viewer to actively participate in the image creation themselves by way of investigation, inviting myriad readings within a given theme.

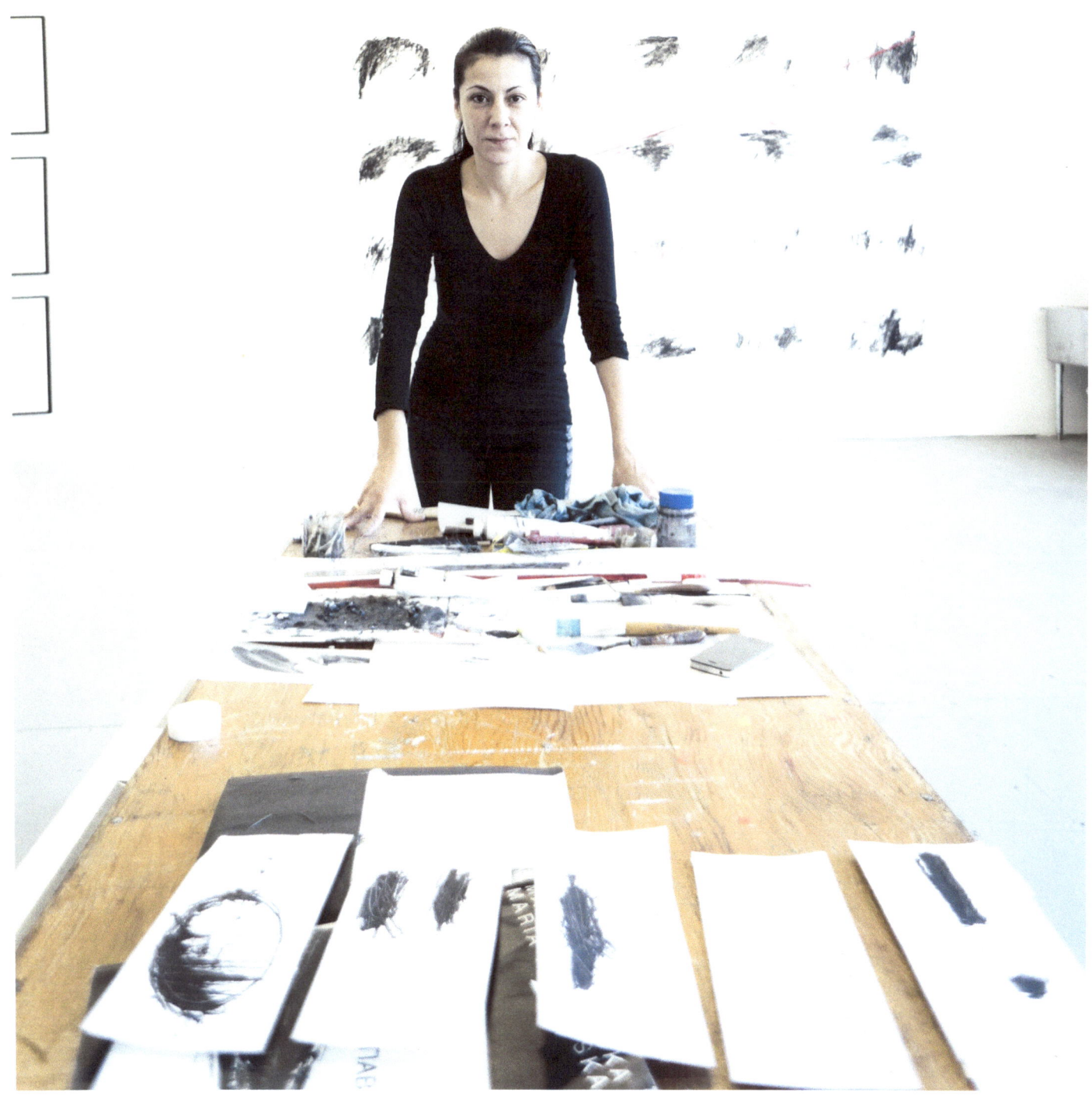

Maria in her studio at MANA Contemporary

# VICTORY HALL PRESS

is a division of Victory Hall Inc.,

a not-for-profit arts organization producing exhibitions, events,

education programs, public projects and publications,

based in the NJ/NY metro area.

Other books include:

## DRAWING ROOMS

*Jill Scipione: Psalms and Prophets*

*Pictures of Everything: Abstract Painting Now*

*The Big Small Show 2014*

## PORTRAIT PROJECT

*Ross Bonn:100 People*

*Ian Charles Scott:: The Shape of the Being*

## NEW DRAWING SERIES

presents series of innovative, current images

from artists whose work explores and expands

the visual and conceptual language of drawing.

*Ibou Ndoye: Forms of Faces*

*Ibou Ndoye: Taarou Adaa*

*Jill Scipione: Skullnotebook*

*Carl Vierow: Detective at Red Castle Pier and Other Drawings*

*James Pustorino: Universechild*

*Hector G Romero: Last Coast Blues*

*Cheryl Gross: Drawings from the Z Factor*

To order copies : victoryhallpress.org

Victory Hall Inc.

74 W 46 St

Bayonne, NJ 07002

www.victoryhall.org

May 2015

Victory Hall Press

ISBN-13: 978-0692436189

ISBN-10: 0692436189

Copyright © 2015

Editor: James Pustorino

website: www.victoryhallpress.org

contact: victoryhall1@msn.com

Front Cover: Maria Pavlovska, Detail: Lyrical Cycle 2008

This program is made possible in part by funds from the New Jersey State Council on he Arts/Department of State,

a partner agency of the National Endowment for the Arts, administered by the Hudson County Office of

Cultural and Heritage Affairs, Thomas A. Degise, County Executive, and the Board of Chosen Freeholders.